The

Truth Eternal

The

Truth Eternal

by

Mata Yogananda Mahasaya Dharma

Daoseva Press

The author asserts their rights to be identified as the author of this work under
the terms of the Copyright Act 1991,
including all text and graphical material contained herein.

The Self Realization Meditation Healing Centres
were founded by Mata Yogananda and Peter Sevananda
and the Daoseva Press are their publishing branch.

ISBN   0 9522734 4 6
British Library Cataloguing–in–Publication Data.
A catalogue record for this book is available
from the British Library.

Typesetting in DellaRobbia and Calligraphic-421
by Daoseva Press.
Printed and bound in Great Britain by
Butler & Tanner Ltd, Frome and London.

I dedicate this book

to all

who thirst for Knowledge

FOR SPIRITUAL TRUTHS

FOR

THEMSELVES AND OTHERS

Mata Yogananda
Mahasaya Dharma

These pages are written simply ~ and I pray are sufficient
for the reader to gain insight and knowledge
of important issues without being hindered
by intellectual ramblings ~ which is not my way.
For I believe simplicity in all
is the path of truth and understanding.
These words are written with depth
for all to read and imbibe.
Other words in other books are written for those
who find simplicity and truth difficult to handle.

SO BE IT

I pray you will hunger for more.

M.Y.

Mata Yogananda
and her work in this lifetime

Mata Yogananda Mahasaya Dharma is
the Founder and Spiritual Head of the
Self Realization Meditation Healing
Centres, and the Alpha~Omega family
who live and work in the U.K. Mother
Centre and the Sister Centres worldwide.

For many Mata Yoganandaji needs no introduction.
From an early age Mataji asked that she may experience and
know all the conditions of life. This she did, travelling through the
trials of life ~ marriage, business, child–rearing , illness and
separation~ to the feet of her Gurudeva, Paramahansa
Yogananda.

Paramahansa Yogananda reawakened Mataji for her spiritual
work in this lifetime. Mataji was asked to teach Pure Meditation,
so that all those who wish to may find Self–Realization in this
lifetime. Mataji was also asked to train souls in order to spread
God's work worldwide.

The Self Realization Meditation Healing Centre was founded
by Mataji so that all in need may imbibe there and receive spiritual
guidance and training from those who have faced similar life
challenges. The Alpha-Omega family who live and work at the
Mother Centre with Mataji's blessing, aim to live a God~Centred
life with unconditional love ~ showing that it can be done.

The Mother Centre's permanent home is in Somerset,
England, and its' work has expanded worldwide. Further, Mataji
has founded Sister Centres overseas, to help spread the light to all
those searching souls wherever they may be.

Mataji is a true Guru ~ her every thought, word and deed is
to spread light and love. Mataji's wish is that this book brings you
the spiritual truth and guidance that you seek on your journey.

Contents

Mata Yogananda and her work in this lifetime	xv
Contents	xix
List of Illustrations	xxiii
Foreword	xxv
Heed These Words Now	xxix
It is the Truth I Speak to You	1
Dearest Souls of God's making	3
Knowledge of Yourself	5
Be of Beauty	6
Envy	7
What Makes a Happy Marriage?	9
Fear not, For All is Well	13
Making a Baby	17
Prayer for a Baby	18
Is Infatuation Love?	21
True Love	23
Respect for Ourselves	25
Why are We Here? What are We Here For?	27
Abortions and Miscarriages	31
Flirtation and Its' Dangers	35
A Work Prayer	36
Work ~ How It Can Help Us	37
An Ancient Prayer	38
Illnesses ~ Dis-eases In General	39
Help	40
What we Sow we Reap	43
Pain and Its' Benefits	47
A Remembrance	49
A Needful Prayer	50
Our Family, Friends and Relations	51

Balancing Your Energies ~ Yin and Yang   53
You Are Special   57
As We Love   58
We All Have The Healing Power   59
Mind Power   63
Is there Security in Life?   65
Don't Chase Your Tail ~ Chase God   67
Is Divorce Wrong?   69
Prayer and its' Outcome   73
How Marriage Works Best   77
A Marriage Prayer   78
Pure Meditation and Meditative States   81
Thinking Prayer   84
We are of all Creation   85
It Seems Impossible   86
We Become That Which we Think and Believe   87
God Is Within   88
Good Posture is Good Therapy   89
Life Is For Living   91
What Is and Where Is God?
   How Can We Find God?   93
Today   94
Making Good Use of Leisure Time   95
Only a Vessel   96
The Rape of Mind and Body   97
Respect for Animals   99
Talk to Your Plants   101
Faith   102
Wisdom of the Masters   103
May I Know   104
Be Peace Makers   106
Turn the Other Cheek   107
Our Relationship With The Medical Profession   109

Taking Responsibility For Our Life   113
Monks, Nuns, Recluses and Communities   115
Making Right Choices   119
Karma and Repentance   121
Changing the World   125
Free Yourself from all Desires   127
Physical and Spiritual Food   131
Is there a Reason for Everything in Life?   135
Are Mediumship and Clairvoyance Needed Now?   137
We Think at the Level that We Are   139
The True Seeing Eye   144
The Eye of Delight   145
Verbal Fasting   147
Fasting from Sound   149
Fasting   151
Sleepless Nights   152
A Place of Rest   154
Prepare to Pass in Peace~Joy   155
Let Your Conscience Be Your Guide   159
The Importance of Concentration   161
The Truth Mirror   162
Let's Keep Our Sense of Humour   163
Knowledge of a Dis-ease: Constipation   165
Homosexuality   167
A Prayer for All   168
What Right Have We to Take A Life   171
A Request   174
Jealousy   175
Chakras ~ how many are there?   177
Go with God   178
Intellect   179
Acknowledgement and Prayer   180
Quality and Respect for Life   181

Relying On Your Self   183
Tragedies and Disasters   185
What Happens When We Pass?   189
Exceptional Talents   191
Doubt Can Destroy Your Faith and Yourself   193
To Solve Addictions   194
Alcohol - Spirit and The Spiritual   195
Surrender and Let God Work Through You   197
Separation   199
"God Only." ~ "Thy Will is My Will."   201
Communication by God~Guru and Disciple   203
Breaking The Cycle of Hate and Distrust   205
Education and Travel are Important   207
Smile at Yourself   208
Finding Balance ~ With Humour   209
Please Help Me!   210
Attunement   211
What is a Guru? How can they help you?   213
What Is and Makes a Good Christian?   215
Be Thankful ~ Be Truthful   217
Dreams   219
How to Know and Love God   221
Modern~day Appliances Do Affect Us   222
I WILL   224
Depression, Despair ~ Maya and Illusion   225
Help Us   226
What is Age?   229
I Pray for Forgiveness   230
Meet Adversity with Love   231
What is Reality?   232
The Second Coming of Christ   235
Index   247
The Self Realization Meditation Healing Centre   253

Beliefs and Aims of the Centre   254
Meditation Evenings ~ Worldwide   256
Arms of the Family   259
Help us Help Others   263
Other Publications by Mata Yogananda
    available from Daoseva Press   265

ILLUSTRATIONS

Mata Yogananda Mahasaya Dharma   141
The Self Realization
    Meditation Healing Centre, Somerset, UK   142
Mata Yogananda Mahasaya Dharma
    with Devotees at Darshan,
        Mother Centre, England, 2002   143
The True Seeing Eye (The Third, or Spiritual, Eye) 144

Foreword

*M*any of us yearn for practical spirituality ~ the Truth Eternal ~ to answer questions that have roamed our hearts since we were children.

A Master Guru can answer them, and guide us forward to health, peace and happiness.

Masters are very rare ~ deservedly so ~ for to achieve Mastery an enormous amount of love, dedication and discipline is required.
Yet through the millenia, the Infinite has sent us the Masters who can help us when we are most in need.
Mata Yoganandaji is such a Master ~ a living example of the Truth Eternal. Thanks be to God.
In this book you will find a loving practical spirituality for all to share. Mataji writes at a depth to feed *each* individual reader in a different way.
As well as answering many oft-asked questions about God, the world, relationships and disease, amongst others, Mataji reveals to us the spiritual *truths* of these matters, and offers both prayer and practical wisdom to guide us forward.

Let Mataji touch your heart ~ and guide you home.

D.W.

Heed These Words Now

" Our days are not for us to ponder on but to work in and with to the good of all of life.

We wish you to make a better world, a better place for the souls of the Divine Creator to work the wonders of their Maker.

The world is bereft of all that is righteous, good and respectful, it is in a darkness that is swallowing up their spirit, it needs the Light of the world to keep this world from disintegrating.

Many times the Masters have been sent with the same message of 'Love each other, help and respect the world and all of life.'

People still need to know that unless they change their ways there will be no more world ~ as such, only desecration and a spirit ~ that is dark.

Pollution of the mind, body and spirit abounds. Only those who listen and try to change *can* be saved.

Destruction will come from the air, but with many souls of Light joining force ~ it may still be saved.

Universal energy ~ Light force ~ Love ~ is the only way to self preservation and world preservation. "

Deo Gratias

A Master

I have written the following pages with full knowledge
that most people wish to gain further information
about life ~ its truths and perhaps, above all,
truths about their SELVES.
There are 'truths' that will never change,
then again, there are also 'truths' of the moment.
If we can but look with honesty
~ and face up to the truth ~ then
the truth will set us free.

Each subject in this book has so many different facets
that it would be impossible to explain each and every one.

Take but *one,* and the truth of that *one* will shine through
to reveal the other sides of it ~ if read deeply enough,
or go back to at a later date and read again.

From my heart ~ to yours these words are written.

As you read these words
feel me there with you
~ saying these words to you

loving you unconditionally

caring for you

aware of you whomever
~ where ever you are.

IT IS THE TRUTH I SPEAK

TO YOU

God's Gifts

are freely given,

Life ~ God's life force, to make our own decisions.

The beauty of the planet Earth,

Animals,

Other human beings,

All that is pure and good ~

which is so much taken for granted

by us all.

Dearest Souls of God's Making,

Heed not the mortal dangers to yourself, rather fear the dangers
that await if you do not take care of your **spiritual** self.

Do not fear the unknown. Put your hand out in faith, open
your heart in the true knowledge of your kinship with the Infinite,
that of sons and daughters beloved beyond compare
to any other mortal love.
Such bliss and peace can be had by letting go
of your pride and ego.

Lovingly you are awaited to feast on the joys of the Divine One.

Infinite Beloved, let me see

myself as I truly am.

Help me to change the things

that need to be changed within.

Show me how to be more loving,

more at peace,

more giving to others,

full of joy in all that I do.

Help me to be more

God like.

Knowledge of Yourself

People are complicated, each and every one of us different, in face, figure, characteristics, and different, in the knowledge that we have gained in our lifetimes ~ *every person is special.*

It is important therefore that we know our TRUE SELVES ~ how we 'TICK' in every way; why we think 'THIS'; why we do 'THAT'; our moods and how we react to outside influences, whatever the nature of them may be. *Do not deny your true self.*

Once we have looked with *complete truth* alongside studying ourselves, we will be able to see and change any unwanted habits that are there, making us a better person and bringing to us more love and peace within.

It is not an easy project though, but once we have seen the necessity of doing this, it becomes much easier and can even be a joy to do.

You will never be at peace until you have acquired this information.

How to do this:-

Firstly you must want to.

Sit quietly when you can and ask for help to achieve.

Then breathing gently, naturally, affirm that you wish to be aware of any parts of yourself that need to be changed.

Then let your mind go free ~ to pick up any thoughts that may come to you.

(The secret here is not to let any thought go because (a) you do not want to see it (if it is not what you like) and (b) you think that what you are thinking does not relate to you personally. These are probably *thoughts* you need to look at in depth.)

Be diligent, and make a time for sitting and asking. Face your true self ~ with truth, and your world will open up to you as a much better place to live, with more ability to understand people and events.

You are a special person
with special talents...know this truth.

Be of Beauty

Every face has a beauty

if the thoughts are beautiful

for

Beauty comes from within

so will show and shine upon the face.

Envy will distort thoughts and face...

so therefore

should not be entertained

for one single moment.

Envy

Envy of any kind will make your life very difficult, and unhappiness will blight you. It makes you dissatisified with what you have, making you *want* more.

We should be thankful for that which we have at present, for always we can find people worse off. Though that is not to say we should accept fully our situation, if it truly lacks that which it *needs* for you or your family at that given time.

You are *here* to overcome the unwanted feelings of envy, jealousy and lust, so, put in their place, love, understanding and patience.

Look in the mirror when envious,
Look again when you give love,
And see how it changes the heart
and face accordingly.

♦

Envy makes ugliness
Love shows beauty

✤

We can all have a beauty
if we have love within us.

❤

Be beautiful

Those who pray

Together

STAY

Together

What Makes a Happy Marriage?

To say that 'all marriages are made in heaven' is simply not true, likewise, 'marriages blessed in church will last' ~ not true, but 'Pray together ~ stay together' is a true saying.

There are several important issues you need to consider. Firstly you both need to be following the same spiritual path if possible ~ and it is. The second is to be able to speak on any subject to each other, openly and freely WITHOUT any arguing or criticism.

With just these two abilities, between you, your marriage or partnership has a very good chance of survival. Without them it could be very difficult.

Quite often you may know a person. Purely as a friend, getting to enjoy their company and coming to trust them before you realize that you love them. This is an ideal situation, for, the physical sexual side has developed last of all. This does not mean NO physical attraction whatsoever, perhaps only of a much lesser degree.

Your partner should be your best friend.

Marriages can break down for many reasons: expecting him/her to be perfect. Trying to *make* them as you *think* they should be. Not understanding that there is a *great* difference between a man's and a woman's reasoning, attitudes, emotions, and needs.

It is very wise to get knowledge of marriage and what it entails beforehand.

You may feel you know *it* all, or, that it is not necessary to know. Well, that's pride and ego ~ which comes before a fall.

Talk to a good friend who is married ~ a wise one, and ask them all the questions relating to being married.

There is a great deal to know.

I always say if a woman knows her man through and through, and likewise the man knows the woman, then you will

One priest or person cannot marry a couple.

They pledge their vows to each other

and marry each other.

Blessings for that marriage can be given,

and vows heard.

Marriages are not made in heaven

They are made on this earth plane

with determination, patience and Love.

If it were not for the marriage certificate

received and required for legal benefits,

there would be more people getting

married under God's skies

with a heartfelt spiritual blessing from

a person of their own choosing.

know EXACTLY what to say or do in any given situation.

Accept each other as you are
NO judgement or hidden criticism
Speak the truth to each other
Be giving to each other
Considerate and kind
Loving to each other
Not forcing the sexual side when not wanted, and do remember that though partnerships/marriages can be wonderful, they need to be constantly worked at day by day, week by week, month by month and year by year.

'What you sow you reap' is true of marriages as well as everything else in life.

Always put God first to reap His dividends
that are there for you.

♥

♥

♥

Fear

into

Faith

into

Freedom

Fear not, For All is Well

My dear one, fear paralyses and strangulates. It closes doors, not allowing faith or positivity to shine through.

Our bodies react to our thinking and suffer ~ our life becomes a LIVING hell.

In one way trepidation, a mild form of fear, is needed to perhaps stop us hurting ourselves, or, making a silly mistake, though in truth this can be more to do with 'gut feeling' and intuition, which we always need to heed.

To be able to tread this earth plane without fear, we need to remember that we are never alone. There is a Divine Power within us that we can call on and pray to for help when in times of great need, also remember this *Higher Power Within* houses what is called God ~ the Christ power ~ the Holy Spirit.

We also have great souls that we know have passed, and *remember*, do work on the higher planes. Knowing that thoughts are energy, and energy ~ positive or negative thought ~ travels, then we can see how easily our transmitted thoughts would be picked up, passed on and dealt with, though not necessarily straight away, but at the correct time and in the right place.

Test this truth, but only with gentle prayer ~ saying of your needs, and then go about your day's work contentedly, aware your prayer/asking has been heard. It always helps to finish a prayer/request with

'God's will be done'
or
'Thy will be done'
or
'Let life's will be done'

Keep faith

and

fear

will

never

enter

your

heart

Whatever we do or say involves more than ourselves.
Change fear into faith with this knowledge.
The Divine Power is of unconditional love, peace, truth, joy
~ there to be 'tapped' by asking ~ in prayer ~ in faith.

This faith is needed by all peoples.

This faith will set you free.

'ASK and YOU WILL RECEIVE'

♥

♥ OM ♥

♥

New or old souls being born

are our future.

They need to learn respect for all of creation.

To know of true Love, of all its' facets ~

and be shown how to give love.

Babies need security to grow

within themselves

They need to learn of peace, joy and prayer

~ so as to get and give the best to life.

To become whole human

beings.

Making a Baby

We all know that a baby preferably comes about during cohabitation. Here I am writing of wanting a baby and preparing yourselves for a baby.

We are welcoming a soul into our womb via the seed of a man. This can be a very lovely time for you both. A special time to share together.

You at first need to look at the reasons for wanting a baby, and see if it is the correct reason ~ as so many may not be. Then pray together asking that this may come to fruition.

When you make love, or just beforehand, think of the desire of (for) a baby (both of you). Then entwine gently and lovingly, without any abandonment or force, for *now* is the time for creation to take place.

You may not realise this, but how you both treat the 'lead up' to a creative act *will* make a difference to you and your new baby soul.

There is a right time and place for conception, so stay relaxed within this knowledge.

Many times babies are conceived while on holiday. Why? Because instead of being overtired, overworked and stressed out, people are relaxed and more ready for the entry of a soul.

Look after your health, no smoking, drinking of alcohol, or too many late nights. Keep yourself fit, watch your food intake, making certain you are getting all the nutrients that you need. Masticate your food well, which means that your digestive system has less work to do. Swim, walk or do Hatha Yoga ~ exercise of some kind is needed.

If you keep yourself healthy in mind, body and spirit leading up to conception ~ during ~ and while carrying the baby, not only will you have a more contented baby, you may find that *that* way of life is well worth continuing with ~ for all concerned.

I believe souls choose their parents, that is why so often children differ in character to each other, though still inheriting

Prayer for a Baby

May we conceive in purity of thought

In pure love between us.

Asking for a soul to choose us

If it is to be

God's will.

We do not worry, nor shall

we hurry with demand towards a baby.

We shall wait patiently, in love

for the soul's choosing of time and place

~ for God's time of conception.

certain aspects of their parents personality. They choose the best for their soul's advancement, not necessarily the BEST parents. So we have rebirths and Karma ~ yet another subject.

I am aware of human nature and science's complexities. I also feel that not all women are meant to bear children, for whatever reason that may be ~ I am not about to play God!

There are many orphans in this world for those unselfish enough and far-seeing enough to see what is spiritually needed for THEM. They may prefer this route, whichever way. It is for life that that soul is with us. It entails hard work, much more giving than taking. And we need to know this beforehand.

Go in Peace.

My God

Keep me from the temptations

of casual relationships.

Of infatuation and its' dangers.

Make me strong

in mind, body and spirit

so that

I do not fall

into the pit of delusion.

Is Infatuation Love?

Much is spoken of love and how we should be loving to each other, which is true, but love is not one word which means one feeling or one expression, for it has many. Infatuation is *not* one of them.

Infatuation is one of the most powerful of emotions which sweeps all clear thinking and decency to one side. It neither has respect or truth, loyalty to others, or even consciousness of any harm being done to the mind, body and spirit. It is such a fierce emotion ~ sweeping aside everything that is in its' way.

This description will help you know and guard against such an emotion, for, many people can think infatuation is love and wish to believe it is.

Love on the other hand is powerful, giving, without sweeping all else to one side.

If you get married out of infatuation
Then it will be too late.

Think carefully and choose wisely.

This emotional power can ruin your life.

Pray hard ~ if you feel tempted

God be with you.

Infinite Beloved

My wish is for True Love

A partner to share my life with.

Help me to choose wisely,

not making a choice by *looks,*

but by the inner quality of that person.

You know of my thoughts and *true* needs.

I lift my 'tray' of needs

up into your loving hands

May my pathway be shown to me

True Love

...'Is a many splendoured thing' so the song goes. This is so true, but still it has to be worked on, and *at **once*** when one is married.

True love is more about giving than receiving. Wishing to understand the person, loving them for what they are ~ as they are. Not wishing to change them, though realising change is needed by both of you. It brooks no criticism or judgement, but all thoughts are pure of that special person.

It is of an emotion that takes us to great heights, makes us feel young, vibrant, and the face has a luminosity that it rarely portrays otherwise.

Often people become friends before finding that theirs is a love for each other. Well, there cannot be true love without a friendship within it, otherwise it would not be classified as true love.

It is interesting to note how it seems easier for someone to love a 'cad' rather than a good person, or, get swayed by 'good looks', rich people, than plain people or poor people. Why can we not take into consideration their *inner being~self,* which is being hidden away, not necessarily intentionally, but still there to find out about.

Take your time - enjoy a relationship - but pause before saying 'I Do' for the rest of your life.

WAIT FOR YOUR TRUE SOUL MATE.

Respect is one facet of True Love

Love

is one facet

of TRUE RESPECT

Respect for Ourselves

Respect is vital for our well being.

Whatever we feel we may have done or said in the past ~ it is now the PRESENT, we need to forgive ourselves and to remember that we are a vessel for the Christ Power, Holy Spirit, God. If we do not respect ourselves, then we do not respect God ~ for we are part of God that dwells within.

The Infinite Beloved forgives you, loves you with unconditional Love, so surely you can see how it harms you if you cannot respect the God within. All that is asked of you is that you forgive any errors, affirm you will do better ~ then *do* your best.

You are not alone in your lack of respect for yourself, many others feel the same way. That is why I write these words *now* to save you doing further harm to yourself and others by your lack of knowledge on this matter.

Affirm that God is within you.

You are truly loved.

There is no separation between you.

Affirm this regularly with concentration and you will find your

SELF RESPECT returning to you.

GO IN PEACE WITH THIS KNOWLEDGE.

Let the body know it is God's vessel.

Let our mind soar into the realms of spiritual awareness,

touching on the bliss of the ONENESS with God

Let our Heart be fully opened to

the expansiveness

of the true meaning of Love.

May we find the God Within in this Lifetime.

Om

Why are We Here?
What are We Here For?

This question has been asked of me many times.

The answer is simple: we are here because we have chosen to be, and what we are here for is to find our
TRUE SELF ~ SOUL~ SPIRIT again.

Let me explain and expound on this. We have many incar-nations that we need to go through to get back to our perfect STATE once more, since we abandoned it by the desire of all things mortal, and thereby loosing our true link with our Higher SPIRITUAL SELF.

It takes a spiritual soul a long time to fall from its blissful contented state, it will likewise, take lifetimes of experiences to rediscover it again, or, it would have done so, if the Masters had not taken pity on us and given us Pure Meditation which paves the way to getting there *MUCH* quicker.

The Bible knew of reincarnation, but it has been withheld so the churches would keep their power over the peoples.

It is also extremely logical that we cannot learn all our lessons in one single lifespan, for, people can get very stuck in their thoughts, ways and habits.

NOW IS THE TIME TO CHANGE ALL THAT.

No one person will be truly happy and content until they find their way back to SELF Realization ~ God Realization, back to our SPIRITUAL STATE.

All that is written here bears no relation to religion, in fact, quite the contrary. In religions, however good they are ~ there is dogma. Here I write truths, logical, common sense ones, but it takes a brave person, possibly a suffering one, to look and widen

God knows us

We need to know **ourselves**.

Use a scalpel, dig out any unwanted thoughts or bad habits,

and get rid of them

before they

try to get rid of your inner *spiritual* self.

IF you work towards this knowledge ~

It will set you free.

their horizons to see THESE TRUTHS that have stood the test of time.

You need knowledge of how to proceed. A spiritual D.I.Y. Kit. It is there in the form of PURE MEDITATION.

Life is short. Look for the TRUTH and it WILL SET YOU FREE.

Whatever religion you have, it does not stop you from gaining knowledge this way ~ if you are brave enough, and desire to know more of the Hows and Whys of your life.

I offer you a new start to

your life ~ why not take it

and TRY IT.

My blessings go to you on your journey.

✦

Infinite Beloved,

I ask forgiveness for any unkind acts

that I may have committed ∼

knowingly or unknowingly.

I ask that my baby is received into loving arms,

and grows in the Divine Light of God to perfection.

I now let this soul go free

to grow.

As I now free myself,

to go forward in peace.

Abortions and Miscarriages

So many couples, single parents and single women have said they find it difficult to come to terms with their loss, whether the act was intended or not. This is very understandable, though once a grieving period is over, to make sure we truly have recovered, we do need to look deeply within ourselves and see if there are any remnants of unwanted grief or guilt left, and if so, why.

I believe we know of our destiny before we come onto this earth plane ~ the big issues like birth and passing from this life ~ but it is obliterated from our minds before being born, so that it does not stint our learning powers and progress. If you can accept this, then you will see that babies will already be aware, without any feeling, when and how their lives will cease ~ in the womb or not. Thereby lies their own progress, whatever they need to learn, for however a short space of time inside or outside the womb.

I can understand why people *want* abortions, but do not agree with it, for, whichever way we look at it we are still taking a life. There is damage done also to the person's mind with guilt, fear, worry; and to the spiritual side of that person, all of which will need to be dealt with after the event.

A miscarriage will leave people with similar conditions of asking themselves did we look after our bodies? Was it our fault by being over~tired? and so forth and so on.

I am not saying you could have done better, but, because of how our minds work pushing thoughts into the subconscious to stay there and ferment, it is best that we give ourselves an honest appraisal once and for all time, so that we can truly get on with our lives without hindrance from the past.

Whichever way a baby is lost, we should give a name to this unborn soul, ask for forgiveness (if we need it) and then for both your sakes let the baby go free ~ from your mind.

Remembering a baby soul

in our prayers is worthwhile

and beneficial to the baby

and yourself.

Do it with Joy, knowing that they are now happy

and you *will* meet again

If you so wish it.

Difficult yes! May take time. Do it because thinking of someone long enough has a *pull* on them. By saying, and letting them go free, they can go forward, like you can, on to their next progressive step.

The love link is never lost, unless we wish it to be so. Likewise we can meet up again on our passing.

I still say that I have four children, even though two have passed on from this earth plane.

Your baby, now being looked after and growing on another plane, will be happy, so be happy with this knowledge ~ make good and enjoy the rest of life.

There is a reason behind everything

Nothing is ever lost

God forgives ALL.

The Principles of spiritual Life are pure in their content.

Do not use the beauty of the flesh to entrap,

rather be it

that your inner light shines brightly,

illuminating your whole Visage

attracting to you all that is good, wise and wonderful.

No harm can then come to you through this way of waiting

with your inner light shining forth

to find a soul mate.

Flirtation and Its' Dangers

How often have we heard those fatal words "I was only flirting" or "flirting is harmless." Excuses? A way out of a difficult situation ~ no doubt.

Over the years I have seen more harm done by casual flirting than I care to remember.

People, teenagers in particular, need to know of the truth that any flirtation is dangerous and can/does lead to rape, unwanted pregnancies and many unhappy relationships.

'They are only young' or 'I didn't know' does not 'hold water' any longer, especially with all the knowledge around us. Perhaps, once more it is easier to say 'I didn't realize' than face facts and the truth.

There are ways of showing that we like a person other than flirting with them, showing cleavage and exposed thigh. In fact, no man or woman worth having likes their would–be partner to act like that, as the maxim goes 'if you can flirt with one then you are liable to flirt with another.'

Youngsters need to be brought up with truth of these dangers and respect for their bodies, themselves and *OTHER* people. Don't think this is old fashioned thinking. It is not. It's the truth that goes, or should do, with the modern day thinking.

Show respect and in return be respected.

A Work Prayer

We give our grateful thanks

for any work that we are given.

In knowledge that occupation of the mind and body

is spiritually progressive for us.

❖

May we do our work

with devotion to doing the best we can.

❖

With love and care to every detail.

So that we may gain the progress and blessings

that may be received from it.

Work ~ How it can Help Us

Very rarely will we die from overwork. Feel tired, get ill, maybe. That's if you do not have Pure Meditation at your 'finger-tips.'

Some work is needed for us all. It not only pays our living expenses, but just as importantly keeps our bodies and minds occupied, giving ourselves respect and a reason for living.

It is *what* work, and the work that we *choose* that is the important factor.

To be 'a square peg in a round hole' workwise can be progressive for a short while, though in the long term disastrous to our own state of mind and our family.

All work of any kind needs someone to do it. One job is just as important as another, having a 'ripple' effect on the whole. Once finding work, it's how we respond to it that matters. Always be creative within any work, doing your best, with doing *better* if you can being the hidden motive ~ being more creative.

The work is out there for everyone.

Some prefer the 'dole' to work ~ sad for them.

Keep positive, pray, and keep looking. You will find work ~ if you desire it.

Have patience ~ know this truth.

WITH A POSITIVE MIND ~ IT NEVER FAILS

An Ancient Prayer

Give me good digestion, LORD,

and also something to Digest

Give me a healthy body, LORD,

with sense to keep it at its best.

Give me a Healthy mind, O LORD

To keep the good and pure in sight,

Which seeing wrong is not appalled

But finds a way to set it right

Give me a mind that is not bored,

That does not whimper, whine or sigh.

Don't let me worry overmuch

About that fussy thing called "I"

Give me a sense of humour, LORD,

Give me the grace to see a joke,

To get some happiness from life

And pass it on to other folk.

Illnesses ~ Dis-eases In General

No one person wishes or wants to be ill or have a dis-ease in any part of the mind or body, unless, that is, we have self-pity and we are looking to bring attention to ourselves.

Some dis-eases can be karmic which need to be WORKED through, though not kept. Others are caused by tiredness, stress through worry and fear, yet again a germ can be caught.

So many varied dis-eases that are there for many different reasons. Some we KEEP for a few days, others we keep for months or years. Yes, we can *keep* them, though, we can also help ourselves to get rid of dis-ease with a desire to do so, and with positive thought and with no time restrictions in our mind.

The truth is that no-one likes to feel that they **do** contribute in any way to their dis-ease. The fact is that when we see that *we* **do**, and at the same time acknowledge this truth, we can also say in TRUTH that we can help ourselves get RID of the disease ~ with prayer and faith and work.

If it's a karmic dis-ease (as you sow so you reap) then you need to work through it until the time for the release of the dis-ease will come.

If it's any other cause you need to keep very positive, and see how you brought or caught this dis-ease and then work once again with prayer, and any other method at hand, to get rid of it.

It's amazing how much we can do for ourselves. Don't leave it all to the medical profession. All pills and medications have side effects ~ however small. Self-help though prayer, positive mind and faith in your abilities **do not**.

We must be sensible about this, sometimes we need help from a doctor. There is also a time when we shall pass into another life. The time inbetween these happenings should be one of peace, love and joy.

Help

Father help me with my mind.

To overcome my pain ~ my dis-ease.

Help me to a positive mind,

to faith, peace within.

To feel your Divine presence

in my life. Help me to see

that I am not alone

in my suffering ~

you are with me.

Thou art One

I am as one

We are ONE ~ FOREVER

Amen

All I speak is truth having worked through some dis-eases myself. I found that with intuition, positivity, prayer, faith ~ that it is possible, even pain can be worked through without fear, by losing oneself in deeper thoughts.

I have noticed, as well as it being a fact, that if a person has pain, and for example there is a house fire, or a bigger prob-lem appears ~ their pain is forgotten.

The mind is very powerful and can be used to overcome pain voluntarily rather than in an involuntary way.

Try it ~ it works

Practise makes perfect.

Sowing well - to reap well

is a just law.

To sow badly

and to reap of that bad sowing,

is also a just law.

Infinite Beloved,

may I sow and reap

truly as it is wished to be

on fertile ground,

so that not only I may reap well

but all others in my light.

Bless my sowing,

Creator of all peace,

light and love.

What we Sow we Reap

Whatever you do, say or think has an effect on yourself and others, and has effects on the following outcomes and circumstances.

Thoughts, words and actions are like 'rolling stones' rolling from us, going, gathering, and ceasing to stop until they can go no further.

Therefore be careful of thoughts, making certain that they are good positive ones, changing them, if they are not of that nature, for, they can 'roll' on gathering momentum in your mind until they possess you ~ which is one way we cultivate good or bad habits, by the power of the mind before action takes place.

Some people also speak before they think. A very bad habit, that, if not broken causes untold harm, annoyance and frustration to many people.

When we speak and before we speak, we need to be aware of what the subject is, exactly what needs to be said, and then last but not least, how we wish to say it. If conveying a message, give full details out, for, but one word put in or taken out, which was not there in the first instance, can change or misconstrue the meaning. I call that 'doing the A to Z'. So many people put their own interpretation into other people's words. I continually find this to be so, and know how very dangerous this can be, for example:~ misunderstanding, wrong times given, even a rudeness can be conveyed by mistake. Not to do this unintentionally means listening carefully, with respect for others, then relaying it exactly as it had been spoken to you ~ not impossible if you try.

The DOING is the ultimate act and once more needs deep concentration whether it be to drive a car or lay a lable. Pay attention, concentrate, do your 'A to Z' and you will feel more respect for yourself, will not have to be reprimanded, and furthermore you will find that there will be fewer accidents likely to

What We Sow We Reap
A Blessing to Know

To know that we can be

Masters of our selves.

We can say and do what we feel.

Make decisions and take full responsibility for them.

To know that we can right our wrongs.

What we become is up to our own self ~ in our own hands.

We can be what ever we wish to be

What a Blessing

happen to yourself and others though faulty attention.

Do remember whatever you think, say or do has its own ENERGY ~ and will go ~ and do.

If a harmful act is done by someone, it will be returned to them somewhere, sometime, someplace.

We cannot get away with anything.

A thought can be picked up

A word possibly misconstrued.

An act to someone else, be it good or bad

WILL RETURN TO YOU.

Since realizing these truths I have always been careful I do my A to Z.

I pray you will do the same.

A Statement

I am not this pain

I am spirit

Working through this pain in this vessel

I shall not fight this pain

I shall accept its presence, though not its lingering ~ to stay.

I shall melt into the pain with full knowledge it will travel and go

leaving me a wiser and more compassionate person.

Pain and Its' Benefits

Pain of any kind, anywhere, is not a pleasant sensation. Most of us have suffered pain sometime in our life and I do wish that it need not be so ~ EXCEPT ~ we progress though painful experiences and pain in general.

Pain helps us to be more understanding and patient with others that have to bear pain. It makes us realize we have a mortal body as our *spiritual vessel* and that we need to look after it.

We have a headache, which makes us aware we have a head and mind within, which needs care, keeping it at peace, not letting our emotions get in the way in our mind, to disrupt. Without pain we would continue in life quite selfishly, I feel forgetting our own needs of the mind, body and spirit, but also the needs of others.

It usually takes a severe disease, that *sounds* incurable before we turn to the Infinite Beloved Power ~ God ~ for help. When we have to do this, we then find there is more in life than 'meets the eyes' and with this, a new understanding, faith and peace descends if we allow it to.

If we had this knowledge and above all faith in the first place, we would not need pain to help our progress. In years to come we shall learn and know this fact ~ except for working out any Karma that we may have incurred, Meanwhile ~

We make ourselves suffer
through lack of this profound knowledge
and failing to put this knowledge with faith into practise.

TRUE KNOWLEDGE OF OUR SELVES

AND

OF THE MORTAL

AND SPIRITUAL LIFE

WILL SET US FREE.

A Remembrance

We are here

to find our True SELF

❖

Self Realization

❖

God Realization

❖

To remember

That

we

are

of

God.

❖

A NEEDFUL Prayer

Help me to chart my own path.

Help my parents to release me,

My friends to understand this need.

My relatives to help ~

not to hinder.

For

I ~ alone ~ am responsible

for

my own path.

Our Family, Friends and Relations

These people are important to us, for they shape what we are to a large extent, so are all other peoples, events and happen-ings. They all, to a greater or lesser degree, make you what you are today. Problems, happy times brought about by them also build our character.

Do remember though, that through all that occurs you can respect, like or love them, but, they have individual SOULS, and must at all time be treated as such for their own mortal and spiritual progress as well as your own.

You are not 'beholden' to anyone, except your self and God. You need to go out from your family (Blood family) to find your own path, do your thinking independently, make your own mistakes ~ to spiritually grow into your real self. To be 'stretched', to find your full potential.

So enjoy your family, friends and relations. Do not expect too much of them. Listen to them ~ above all respect them ~ their inner qualities, for, everyone has one, two or more. Then do what you say and feel is right for *you* at that given time.

Any person, whomever, who tries to manipulate our life, should not be listened to ~ they are dangerous people. Take advice, listen to wisdom, then *make your own mind up, taking full responsibility for your actions ~ and from them grow.*

Yin and Yang

balance

harmony

nature

love

Divine Father,

*may **all** be within me*

Balancing Your Energies
Yin and Yang

It is known that anything alive has energy within it. One Energy with 'offshoots', going into different forms of life.

The human species is of wonderful creation. The body having all it needs to make it work perfectly, unless, there is disharmony and an imbalance of its energies.

I could write with many long words used on this subject, but prefer to keep it simple, for all *minds* to digest, for simplicity of speech and in writing will, I pray, let truth and sincerity through.

So, we are energy, energy can produce sound and light, so can we.

Our bodies use energy. Energy for our brain to work, our minds to function. For the digestive system, our heart, kidneys and liver. All parts of us need energy to live. To be healthy we need to know this, and look after the workings of our body by proper exercise; rest; *good* food alongside good eating habits; keeping an active brain.

Bearing in mind all this, there are some parts of us that play 'havoc' with us: our minds, when they lack concentration and our emotions, used in the full sense of the word, that can tear us to pieces with anger, jealousy, envy, impatience, infatuation ~ to name but a few.

These all give out energy, take it from our body, and being. Negative energy manifests to harm us.

Over~stimulation or excess of certain chemicals within, bring about an imbalance in some form or another. Whichever way it is said or written ~ OUR ENERGIES ARE NOT BEING BALANCED ENOUGH.

Like a car, we need to keep 'a gentle' eye on its workings, give it an M.O.T. occasionally. The secret here is not to be overly concerned, only give the body its due.

Beloved one,

May our energies be balanced

The yin and yang become

OM

allowing the mind, body and spirit

to flow in harmony

and purity.

Each body is different, and will be, according to our upbringing and lifestlyle, so, what is good for one body, may not be good for another. Which means you should get to know what works best for YOUR body, then, use your intuition when dealing with it. Only you know how you feel, what your body is saying to you.

When it speaks, listen to what it is telling you, ask for advice if needs be, then go on your own intuition and deal with it. Then forget about your body, for too much time spent in this way does more harm than good.

Our M.O.T. should consist of seeing if we are at peace, in our minds, for, if our minds are peaceful, our bodies should be. Look at your food and food intake, do go for walks, a swim, Yoga! Is your mind healthy? - try to keep it positive at all times.

If not you need to Meditate more. If you do not Meditate then take time out to sit quietly and do some breathing exercises.

Keeping the mind and body in the best condition that you can, and at peace with your whole being, will mean your energies are well balanced.

You may be working out karma, have aches and pains, still you need to look and balance.

On the spiritual path, before you reach another LEVEL the body can play up ~ to detoxify itself, so that it can keep up with your spiritual progress ~ *do remember this.*

We cannot expect perfection, but with faith and common sense we can get pretty well near to it.

There is a Divine Energy that we can call on when we need a helping hand. Pray ~ ask for help.

Why not?

The unreality is life

The True Reality is God

You Are Special

Yes, **you** are very special. There is no one person exactly as you are, perhaps somewhat the same, but that is all, they will never be completely the same.

You are unique, having the Christ Power and Holy Spirit within ~ you are made in God's image. What is just as important to know is that each and every one has the potential of finding *God within*. Becoming more God like each day, until one day we realise that there is no separation in life. We *know* that we are God ~ all is God.

You are the stars, the moon, the sun, you are of all creation - and that is why you are a special soul. Loved unconditionally ~ understood unconditionally ~ by God and Guru. Therefore you need to understand, have patience, and love your TRUE SELF ~ forgive yourself, your failings, while you try harder to change the outer layers of ego and pride of unwanted emotions, all, of negative nature, into a positive loving energy which is the God within, just waiting for **you** to peel off the skins of unreality. To find the peace, joy and love that is *there within.*

How can we afford *NOT* to love, respect, have patience with ourselves, and,

forgive our lack.

As We Love

May our love heal,

may our light shine brightly

~ so others in need may receive.

As we walk this earth plane, may our beacon of light

~ of the healing power ~ through our love of all creation

GO FORTH AND HEAL

We All Have The Healing Power

To say otherwise would be to acknowledge, incorrectly, that some persons are above others. This is not so. What can be said, is, that not everyone is aware that they have the ability to heal, or perhaps they do not wish to explore this avenue of thought.

Healing is a loving positive energy. Used with sincerity and a desire to help, it goes out from a person as a smile, an acknowledgement, having a listening ear to other people and their problems, or, equally, just being still, calm, allowing that state to be seen by and imbibed by others. Sharing a laugh, looking content with a gentle smile on your face ~ all these outward manifestations have a certain amount of healing energy within them that is picked up by others.

You do not have to think about giving healing in this way, in fact, it is best you do not. Let it happen naturally, without thought, and those around you will receive and feel better for the receiving.

If you hurt yourself or have a pain put both your hands on that area, and ask for the healing power to help you.

It will.

You can lie down, breathe gently in and out, asking as you do this that you may receive a healing, and stay, letting this Divine energy feed you, until your intuition tells you that you have received.

Give thanks, get up, and **close over** well using the Blanket Covering. This is a simple and, if done with concentration, extremely effective scientific way of covering over. Use your mind ~ concentration ~ to see a blanket or a blind lifting from the base of the spine and up **in front** of the body, to the top of the forehead. Mentally leave it there. Do not take it over the top of the head.

If you need to attach it somewhere, the top of the forehead

will be the place for this. This Covering Over **conserves** our energy.

You will now see what I mean about giving and receiving this bountiful energy that *is there* for us to give and receive.

Be as a lighthouse, beaming light out of love, peace, joy, patience, understanding, helping souls who, if it were not for that light shining ~ would go astray, get hurt ~ or just be lost in the dark. Do not let this happen, you have enormous light energy to spare.

So go forth and

spread the light.

Do we Know

the great power of the mind

when at one with God

~ brings forth a power that works natural miracles

~ moves mountains, controls the elements.

Purity of mind is needed above all for such a gift of this power.

PURITY

of mind is needed......

Mind Power

What is mind power? It is conscious mastery over thoughts and actions bringing about whatever is to be said, needed or done at any given moment.

When you have this 'mastery', the discovery is made of how powerful the mind is, and we are also aware of the powerful energy that is *within us* . It therefore goes without saying too much about it, that most people will not be able to find their mind power completely before they redress their pride and ego. Turned loose, such a person who has not done this, can be, and is, very dangerous to themselves and others.

Business Tycoons, people of genius, plus many more have found this 'power' to a degree in one facet or another, tempered with ego and pride. If used with wisdom and caring thought, then, this mind power can move mountains, subdue raging waters and prevent us making human errors of many kinds.

First seek for the kingdom of heaven (of truth, love, peace and your spiritual growth within) and then all shall be added to you, meaning you will be unable to do harm to others, so you can receive this mind power ~ if you so wish.

Use it for the benefit of others, for, to use it *completely* for self interest will dilute the power with possible harm to your self ~ your bodily energies.

**Energy ~ power ~ is not to be played with
~ you do so at your own risk.**

Security within

will come

when you know

without a shadow of a doubt

that God manifests

from within.

Security of the SELF,

the God within,

IS THE only

True Security

that you need.

Is there Security in Life?

However sad is this fact ~ there is no security for us in this life, with regards to money, family or friends. We may think that by building up our finances, our gathering of friends around us, plus husband, wife or children, that these will stay with us bringing us security.

At any moment they could be taken from us.

Nothing really belongs solely to us. It is bought, given or lent to us. A special vase can get broken. A car wrecked, a child dies, a partner leaves. It is best we do not get *overly* attached to people or things for this reason. Let us love our family and friends, remembering that they are individual souls who need, in fact ~ must ~ be allowed complete freedom to travel their own path, be it with you, or without you.

Having given the truth which is of *insecurity* , now, let me give you the truth of a security that you can accept.

That is the security that God and Guru cannot let you down, though you may have your doubts, they are *your* doubts only. So we can bathe in this security with the knowledge that *this* will never change.

Isn't that the very best security of all.

Through Self~Realization

all your needs will be met.

And later still

with your complete faith and devotion

your wants

~ if they do not harm your spiritual progress ~

will also be realized.

Don't Chase Your **Tail**
~ Chase God

I believe that Albert Einstein, the German physicist and philosopher once remarked:

"I want to know God's thoughts ~ the rest are details."

How right he is, though, to know God's thoughts are also to know our own. To work firstly with our own thought, delving deeply within, having Pure Meditation to help us, we can, and will, eventually learn more of God's thoughts. This comes to pass by desire to learn and know. Devotion to the task, and faith in the achievement of the task, perseverance and patience being paramount.

Much wasted time is spent on 'chasing our tails'. We run around collecting all manner of friends, objects, money. We try all sorts of different jobs, move house often. Eat, work, play, sleep. Our desires, our wants, we chase forever. But, we do not CHASE God:
The one thing that is needed to make our life complete ~ our SELF whole:
The very ingredient that will bring peace and harmony into our life.

You cannot live life fully without this one ingredient.

You will only exist primarily in the mind and body. You may not agree but one day you will find this out for yourself.
I know for I have lived both parts of these lives, and know it to be true.
You don't have to 'chase God' too hard for God is within just waiting for you *to seek ~ **and you will find.***

Think long and hard

before entering into a divorce.

♦

If both are willing to talk

and change, then there is a

chance of reconciliation.

♦ ♦

If not, part amicably

~ as friends, so that no harm is done

to your selves or others

♦

Pray for help. Listen well.

You must judge for yourselves~

and *then* take *responsibility* for your *actions*.

Is Divorce Wrong?

Well! Let's look at the truth of the matter. One minute we are led to believe that God is all loving, wishing us to be happy, healthy and enjoy this lifetime. In the next minute we are told (by the churches) that divorce is wrong.

Would a loving God expect two people who fight and do not get on, who are probably inwardly, in spirit, very unhappy, to stay together? I think not. Certainly they should not give up on their marriage straight away, but give it time by each doing their best to put matters right. If after several years they find that their situation is getting worse and not better, then, for their own progress as well as those around them, particularly where children are involved, it would be better if they did divorce, perhaps enabling the two when apart from each other to become better friends. If done in a spiritual way, without rancour or meanness, then if children are involved ~ being how resilient they are ~ it could prove the best situation for them in the long run.

So in certain circumstances divorce is necessary and best for all concerned.

Many people marry when they are too young. They lack life's experiences and because of this have not found their own true identity, so therefore grow apart as time goes on. Some marry at a very young age and it is a success, but this is not the norm.

I believe that to get married is good, but only when two people are absolutely sure that they can be good friends as well as lovers.

No one has a right to judge others, only to give 'open ended' advice, if asked, as to what is best.

We need to remember that each person is an individual with a soul, here on this earth plane to find their true selves and path in this life time. If it's not possible with their present partner, then it's inevitable that a separation will come about.

Infinite Beloved.

help us to make

the right decisions

for ourselves,

our family and for

all concerned,

so the outcome will be

spiritually progressive

with no harm done.

Unfortunately separation is used as an easy option these days. More guidance is needed, more information on marriage, children and possibly divorce and the intense suffering that it can bring to all involved.

Will people in love, or, those that think they are in love, listen to the advice of others? Would you? It can be very difficult for them ~ when the emotions are high.

I believe that the majority of couples should wait until they reach an age of discretion before embarking on such an important step in their life as marriage, and certainly should not do so in their teenage years.

Divorce should not be taken lightly

and entered into at a whim.

Prayer can move mountains

Prayer is all powerful.

By praying you are

calling humbly on the

Divine Energy to help you.

Heartfelt prayer can move all

obstacles, change people.

It is the most powerful source

and as such you should use with love

and respect at all times.

Prayer and its' Outcome

People say why pray to God if God is within us?

There are many reasons why we need prayer in our lives. It is an outlet for us when things go wrong. We feel with prayer that we are being heard and that help is at hand, also it keeps a humbleness within us.

We need prayer and to pray ~ it does not need us. Let me outline the full picture for you.

We have a body housing the mind and spirit, the spirit separating from the body on our Passing.

We have a soul within. This is housing our Godlike quality of pure love, light. Our level of spiritual development will determine how much of God we are (light~love~wisdom.)

We may need to peel the skin (pride and ego) from the kernel to find the completeness of God within. Meanwhile, our spirit (our higher self) does help us with this advancement if we use our intuition and listen to it. This *is* our higher self.

When we pray, in some ways we are actually praying to our higher self which in turn is heard in the ether (being that prayer houses energy) by the Masters, enlightened souls. They, being more advanced spiritually have the knowledge and wisdom of how to help us ~ and what we need. These souls can PETITION for us.

Think of God, as God is 'omnipresent' ~ there being within a storehouse of endless understanding and unconditional love ~ containing everything for every single person, and just waiting in the omnipresent for each one of us to acknowledge our true SELF and God as ONE.

Pray and ask in faith that you may receive, and you will receive.

It doesn't matter how you receive or when ~ just know that you will do so at the right time ~ and in the right way. For there is a right time for everything.

Pray for us Infinite Beloved

as we pray to you.

❧

Keep us humble in mind, body and spirit

As we acknowledge our needs outwardly in prayer.

☪

The heavenly planes are well organised, it has to be so. Don't demand or plead, ask as a child of God, then leave the rest up to God and the wiser souls.

The answer to your prayers more often than not will arrive from someone, or seemingly normal happenings, a *miracle* appearing *normally*. **God and Master souls do not like to boast or 'show off' their powers.**

So be humble, pray, give thanks for all you have ~ or *have not*. Don't be afraid to ask in prayer ~ when you have tried everything ~ done your best ~ and truly are in need.

You will receive.

Marriages are not made in heaven.

They are made by two people

who make their vows to each other.

The whole responsibility is theirs

to make the marriage work.

We need a marriage certificate for legal documentation only.

The vows you make to each other are the most important.

How Marriage Works Best

Marriage is a very deep commitment and should not be taken lightly.

Far be it for me to know how all marriages work best. I do know of certain attributes that are needed to make a good partnership.

During my years of counselling married couples, it seems to be lack of communication between them, not having quality time together, and their inability to understand and accept their partners needs that are amongst the main problems.

If our partner is our best friend first and foremost, allow time for discussion on important issues, be it of money, children or ~ "who has been using my toothbrush?", which may sound a miniscule thing, but, it is the seemingly 'little things' in marriage that can cause the most upsets. If two people can speak together reasonably without showing anger and frustration, begging to differ at times, then there is a reasonable chance that the marriage will succeed.

Religion is another way marriages can get torn apart. If possible it is much easier and better to be of the same religion and same background if possible.

Being of ages near to each other also means you have experienced the same era and gives more common ground ~ allowing more to talk about.

I have heard the argument that some marriages may best be conducted by living apart half the time, or, that 'arguments make our marriage work' or still again 'that without the sexual side, our marriage would not last'. All I had to say to the latter remark is that this marriage is built on 'stony ground' and at some stage in their life ~ for whatever reason that it may be ~ the sexual urge should grow less, unless, with pride, we try to keep it alive (very tiring and unproductive.) As our hormones change, so should our

A Marriage Prayer

Infinite Beloved

May we bless ~

and be blessed upon our marriage.

May the light of true love

be with us and manifest more

so as we travel this path

together

may wisdom and unconditional

love be used by us in

all that we do.

relationship, becoming *less* sexual, turning into a deeper phase of friendship. If either tries to keep it alive in the latter years, then it probably means that there is insecurity and necessity to prove oneself.

Sexual relationships can become like a drug ~ wanting more and more variation.

Sexual activity in marriage can be made beautiful and is a bonding between couples, though not actually a *neccessity* to accomplish this.

In the beginning we used thought and breath to produce life.

Now we have to use sexual intercourse to produce babies (if we are meant to have them, or adopt if we are not).

When we reach an age when our hormones say ~ 'that's enough', then we should listen, and let the deep friendship within our marriage take over. Marriage then may become less passion-ate, but it also becomes more peaceful, less demanding, giving you more time to look at the spiritual side and more realistic side.

Take time, choose wisely and carefully.

And remember in most marriages there is nearly always one partner that loves and gives more that the other. Perhaps that is the way it works best.

'Pray together, stay together' is often true.

ॐ

The fruits of the earth

are like nectar to our taste buds

The trees, flowers and nature

in all its changing seasons

are there to give us succour.

Pure Meditation is there

to set free our spirit,

clearing our mind of all unwanted waste.

Expanding our heart and mind

to see more clearly on all life and that which it has to offer.

Granting us more peace, love and joy.

Pure Meditation
and Meditative States

Any form of Meditative State is worthwhile to a degree. Whether it be sitting in the candlelight breathing gently, walking with a Meditative mind or just sitting under a tree watching all of nature. There is some good in most of the states of being whereby we are pausing for rest and thought.

Seriously think what you are wanting to receive from this moment of time. If it is to relax and feel peaceful and no more, then, it's all to the good, but if you still feel bereft of 'something', though you cannot gauge what it is, then Pure Meditation could be for you.

There are many forms of Meditation; Transcendental Meditation; Zen Meditation to name but two, and all these are here varying in some form of another, thus giving a variety for people with different tastes and needs. Also they are there to meet people's different levels of spirituality. This is how it should be ~ at this present stage of evolution.

Now it is time for the heightening of spirit within the human race, bringing with it discontentment to the level that that person is at. The spirit (person) will need more 'food for thought' ~ will wish to delve deeper into themselves and the meaning of life.

This is where Pure Meditation comes into its own.

In all my years studying the different forms of Meditation, I have to say, not one other has incorporated everything that has been needed to satisfy and allow a person to take responsibility for themselves *and* at the end of a guided course in Meditation have a 'Do It Yourself' kit to last them for the rest of their lives.

Pure Meditation does this by having such a comprehensive D.I.Y. Kit to fulfil *all* your needs. Handed down through the voice of the Masters, always at a time when this earth plane is in great

NOW is the time for all of humanity

to know that God is within.

Don't waste every precious moment

left in your life wondering.

Look and find God within ~ find your true self

and God~like nature NOW,

before it is too late,

and you *pass* in ignorance

of the *truth* — that sets you free.

need, it is a spiritual way to find your true Self, Self~Realization and God Realization.

Also incorporating Raja and Kriya Yoga, the teachings are on all aspects of life. We need these teachings in our life now as never before.

It is a Jewel in the Crown of the Infinite Beloved.

Thinking Prayer

Let us think good creative thoughts

~ to become a good creative person.

Let us believe in our self ~ our abilities.

Respect and love our SELF

acknowledge we are an important part

of the whole Divine Plan.

Let us remember

we can be as one

with all of creation.

We are of all Creation

There is an energy link connecting us to all of life. That is why we need to understand that this one link ~ if only THIS link ~ means all the world of human beings are family, descending, multiplying and developing in different beliefs, ways and attitudes in many different parts of the world.

Some living now are very new souls, others not so new, whilst some are old souls. They can be recognised if we look deeply into their psyche and not just at them.

Rather than do this it is best to accept that every one person is here for a reason. They have a path to tread. However good or evil they may appear to you to be, there is a kernel (however small and unseen) of good ~ God ~ spirit ~ within them.

We are also part of the Universe, the moon, sun, wind, plants, animals. All these parts of the Universe have energy and a life~force, which we can feel within, from time to time. Certain people, perhaps, will be more sensitive to this energy than others, or sensitive to it without the realisation of why. The new moon and full moon; the wind; the sea; they all give out vibrations of different energy at different times. These different times can help or hinder us if we are not Master of our mind and body.

The full moon can make one restless. We can pick up invigorating feelings of energy from the sea and its' ozone. And do we not pick up feelings of anger, despair or excitement, to name but a few, from people? This is because we do have this earth and cosmic energy link. There is One energy/light and numerous offshoots, like water and electricity, they can be used in many ways, for the good, or ~ for harm.

When you give it thought you will realise. Our bodies contain a good percentage of liquid, light, energy. Sometimes we can give or receive an electric shock from static electricity.

Science has much more to discover and make us aware of.

There is one thing that will never be discovered ~ cut up ~ dissected and explained by science, and that is our spiritual self, soul.

Thank God for that.

It Seems Impossible

Help me to see that

all things are possible with prayer

◆

Humbly I pray for the wisdom of the Masters,

to my Guru to see my

way forward to solving this problem ~ for the good of all

Thy will be done

We Become
That Which we Think and Believe

Thought is a very powerful medium. If we think of an idea, perhaps of being a good painter, and really believe that we will be able to achieve this desire, then we will.

I have seen people make themselves unwell with the belief they are going to be. Likewise there are those I have also noticed, that have made themselves well overnight. Placebos are given by doctors in certain trials that have proved this to be so.

You have a vast computer within, housing all knowledge and most abilities from which we can extract conscious and subconscious information when we wish to.

I'm not inferring that we all can be a genius at everything, but we can be pretty good at most things ~ if we have a desire to be so.

I have used this 'recall' on many occasions when a job has had to be done straight away when I have never done it before ~ and it works.

So THINK ~ BELIEVE ~ THEN ACT

God Is Within

Stand balanced well in body.

Stand up for God.

Sit in posture when seated,

to show what God can do.

Walk tall

and the God~like quality

will be noticed.

Sleep well relaxed

in mind and body,

to feel

God's blessings.

Good Posture is Good Therapy

Have you looked around you recently and seen the number of people who hunch their shoulders, push their heads down and forward in a 'tackle' position? Walk with hands in both pockets and never seem to stand upright? I have never seen so many people with bad posture ~ for a very long time. They may be able to give a valid reason for doing so, but, the untold harm it does to them over the months and years will be enormous.

If you develop a good posture, you will feel better, look better and have a feeling of self worth. People will notice this *new* you, will show more respect to you when you have your head held high ~ as you show respect for yourself and you show a powerful posture.

Our body will respond with better health, for walking or sitting with a slumped body whereby our intestines, our spine, our organs, are all being pushed down on top of each other ~ all gravitating DOWN instead of helping our body to gravitate up, can only lead to body problems.

Stand before a mirror, stomach IN, shoulders in good position, head level, then lift up gently from the waist, find *your* proper posture. Bodies are different, you may be leaning too far forwards or backwards, see if you can adjust it yourself ~ or get advice if uncertain.

Don't cross your legs when sitting. This can hinder circulation. Sit with the base of your spine well into the back of the chair. Find the chair that is most suited to you.

Watch how you place your feet and hands. See they are comfortable.

Our body is an indicator of how we truly are, how we are feeling, and other people do notice and respond to us accordingly, probably without you even being aware of it ~ or why.

Correct your bodies' balance, get your deportment as it should be. You will be pleasantly surprised of the difference that it makes to you and your life.

LIVING LIFE

Every minute of your life

is precious.

Make the most of every second;

every minute every hour;

for they will not return again for you.

Your mind, body and spirit

has been given to you to treasure

and enjoy life with that knowledge.

We pass this way but once,

a facet of one life completed.

By making the most of your time,

enjoying every minute,

when your life is finished

you will have no regrets.

Life Is For Living

I do believe fully that you should learn how to enjoy every minute of this lifetime.

The faces full of joy are few, the sad long faces are many. We have to realise that the life span is short, so, it is up to each and every one of us to make the very most of it.

There are wars, famine, murder, rape, inter-family fighting, even small children using violence as a way of life.

How can we be joyful in such a world?

The answer is to acknowledge that all this is happening (that's the truth) but then do not dwell on such things for they will manifest in your mind if you do so. These can become a full-time talking point, and also lead to feelings of depression.

Talking about events of a horrific nature does not help matters, in fact quite the reverse.

Prayer is needed. Being helpful when needed. Above all we need to rise above this bad negative energy. We do this by a smile, bringing upliftment and joy to those around us, and keeping faith that there is a reason for everything. Countries and people are working out much of their own karma now. Eventually good will prevail. Meanwhile, play your part in life by living life fully with faith and joy.

The only difference beween

saints and sinners

IS

that saints know God is within

and sinners do not.

Our spirit will never rest

'till

it finds its way home

to God

THAT

IS

THE TRUTH.

What Is and Where Is God?
How **Can We** Find God?

There is only ONE GOD, called by many different names depending on one's religion.

That there is a God is the most important fact. God is omnipresent, omniscient, IS, always has been, always will be.

Everything must come from somewhere and end up somewhere, yet in spiritual life there is no beginning and no end ~ just a ~ BEING. You may believe in the Darwinian theory, but it doesn't hold ground! For our bodies are so perfect for the task in hand. And what is the point in life and living if there is no 'outcome' to it.

We can make of God what we will 'TO BE OR NOT TO BE', nevertheless,

GOD IS.

God is everywhere within every one, every living organism. The fact that we don't understand, realize or maybe not want to accept this fact, does not make it *untrue*.

To find God is more difficult, unless we can acknowledge there are many things we will never completely understand, and much still to learn. We find God though faith; through the blessing of a so called miracle happening to us; through prayer and the desire to experience God; by Pure Meditation.

The *knowing* comes in many different ways to people. We shall not be truly content and peaceful 'till we *do* find God.

Today

Today we shall walk by the sea

smell the ozone, listen to the seagulls.

With hands entwined, we shall feel

the love between us

and glory at the wonderments

of nature.

♥

Making Good Use of Leisure Time

Too much leisure time is not good for us. It can make us inclined to be lazy in the mind as well as the body.

We do need time off to balance, in what ever way is needed at that particular time. More importantly it is not the amount of time that will give us balance, but the QUALITY.

If energy is wasted by our talking, demanding behaviour, arguing, then, that valuable time is being wasted. If, on the other hand, intuition is used beforehand to determine what is needed for you at that time, and then acted upon, you will find the day will go well, bringing to you joy, peace, and upliftment. Occasionally you may need to let your hair down ~ do as you want, be a little careful NOT TO GO 'over the top'. I do not advise this too often for a bad habit could ensue.

A great many people do not know how to get the best of their leisure time, and the way it shows is by seeing them the day after, when they should be content and feel renewment in their mind and body, but they are not feeling so, only tired, edgy, and impatient to name but a few ailments.

You have to learn this art form, for, that is what it is. Once you have this knowledge all of your leisure times will be well spent, and of great value to you.

IT IS BOTH WHAT you do

AND HOW YOU DO IT

that matters

Only a Vessel

Our body is just a vessel

for our mind

and spiritual self ~ soul

When we leave this earth plane

our soul sails forth

Our body may be TAKEN.

It cannot be sullied

only, if, we let it be in our own minds,

will it be so.

Remain pure in mind

and you will be PURE.

God loves us.

The Rape of Mind and Body

I do not like the word 'rape', yet, it has to be used. Much is heard about it these days. A vast subject with many facets which I do not intend to go into. There is, though, an important facet that is important to write about.

We have a mind, a soul, a body. If there is a rape of the body, it will affect the mind but *not* the spirit~soul.

The person who has effected this rape *will* have their *spiritual higher self* affected, in fact, that person will reap much bad Karma which they will suffer for in due course.

The most important thing to know is this:– providing that a person themselves has not incited a rape in any way, then, though a body rape takes place, and that person may feel 'dirty', no-one can touch or harm our soul *unless we allow it to happen*.

What we cannot prevent, we are not guilty of.

Though rape of the body is terrible and wrong, in my eyes the rape of the mind is much worse. This is done not only with torture (as during wars), but also done by a seemingly ordinary person who wishes harm to another and usually is not mentally balanced.

I saw this act being deviously done to a relative. It was cunningly done and constant, so much so that this relative wondered what was happening to her and if she really was going mad. I was young at the time and though seeing the horror of it did not understand completely what was happening. Fortunately, the relative was strong-willed, saw the situation and sent the person who was trying to rape her mind 'packing'. If she had not done so the consequences could have been dire.

I am not belittling any form of rape, but mind rape is much more difficult to get over than a bodily rape be it continuous or otherwise.

If we cannot prevent our mind being raped,

perhaps not our body,

our soul can never be raped

without our sanction.

I knew of a lady who had a very lively kitten given to her, the kitten would play with her which annoyed her, so she 'tapped' it with her hand and the kitten with its paw responded likewise. It clawed at her armchair so she 'tapped' the kitten again, likewise the kitten kept responding by 'tapping' back. This lady got angry with the kitten and told me that she did not like the kitten as it would not do as it was told. Therefore I suggested that she used a strong tone of voice with the kitten instead of smacking it ~ to show respect for it and its needs. Also, to give the cat a few playthings and to include a tree that she could scratch her claws on.

This being done, it took a little time for *both of them* to behave, but eventually they became the best of friends, both giving each other the respect that they deserved.

Respect for Animals

This statement is deeper than it sounds or reads.

People make pets of animals for different reasons; companionship; love; ownership; guarding a house; sometimes because they are prepared to give to human beings unconditional love, loyalty and do not answer back. Whatever is the reason, if we treat one like a human being we are asking for trouble for ourself and a distortion of life for that animal.

Animals and their instincts need to be respected. Let them show you what they need from you, allow them to show you, by their attitude, if they feel like being 'fussed' or not, are hungry or not. Do not force them to accept ALL human ways.

By having respect for each other, you both will get the very best from the relationship.

Of course dogs, for example, who sit on cushions with bows in their hair may seem a good idea to you, they can't complain easily, and have to accept it, but, I wonder how they truly feel!

Try to reverse the situation and see how you would feel.

Animals can show how they feel, what they need ~ watch, and make a true contact with their eyes and mind. They do pick up on your feelings and state of mind. Learn to do the same so that an animal can be respected for what they *are* ~ not made into what *you think* they should be. By doing this both you and your pet will go forward in a mortal and spiritual way to a very loving relationship. Though I do hope you are able to give your love and loyalty to human beings at the same time ~

for all are God's creatures

great and small.

$\mathcal{M}$ay all who pick flowers

see that some wish to stay,

others to be happily picked.

They are best left to reflect on,

while they stand majestic,

swaying in a gentle breeze,

bringing delight to our heart,

tranquility to our senses.

Talk To Your Plants

My dear ones love your plants and talk to them. They will respond by growing and living longer.

They have energy and can give of this energy, so do we; and if we truly love and wish our plants well ~ from the heart, then, the vibration of this energy will be felt by the plant to a larger or lesser degree depending on the different species of plant life involved.

Plants do have a 'shelf life' like humans, but, many a so-called 'dead' plant has been nurtured back to life.

I love buying plants that look sick ~ to love them back to a healthy state. To feel that many plants are discarded that could be saved is saddening to me.

Of course you can show them too much love by over-watering or handling them too much. We need to use balance in all that we do. Don't forget to hug a tree when you can. From the tree outwards to a distance of a few feet there is an energy ring, which, on hugging the tree and communing, we will receive energy and upliftment. Don't forget to bless the tree (energy freely given to you) or at least say 'thank you'. For in everything that we receive there is also a giving ~ or should be. Duality is in every-thing.

I always, before I pluck a flower from the earth, wait 'till there is a feeling within of which flower is the one to pick and take. I am fully aware that it is possible to 'make believe' on this matter, though if given careful thought, the intuition comes into play, and it works very well for me.

So why not for you.

Faith

Forgive us

any of our sins

that we intentionally,

or unintentionally do,

as they offend thy Infinite Goodness.

May we put any wrongs ~ to right.

So no Karma is reaped

by your loving devotee,

who prays here before you

most Infinite Beloved.

Wisdom of the Masters

Masters have come to us down the ages, since time immemorial, with messages for that era of time. Whatever has been that message, it has always included messages of love and truth;

'Love others as you would be loved'

'Do unto others as you would be done to.'

'Respect thy Father and Mother'

These were, and still are words of wisdom and joy, upliftment from these wise souls, tempered with words of encouragement. Then follows the truth ~ that we need to look within, find our TRUE SELVES ~ the God within ~ 'and all shall be added unto you'

I have found this from my own experience to be very true and worth the effort.

When there are troubled times ahead, a Master will be born, once more to help all those souls who are ready and willing to listen. A great many will not wish to listen, will say there is no such person "and never has been", for their own ego and pride will be 'riding high'. They say "we can find our own way" or "I'm a Christian" and don't believe or are not **allowed** to believe.

So, I ask, what about Jesus? What does 'Christian' mean? A person who believes in a Christ Power! Most people at heart have Christ beliefs so therefore are Christians ~ in God's eyes. It's the Church that would have us believe otherwise.

Master Souls come to help us, yet, they get rejected, stoned and crucified. Why?
Because they speak the truth and some people find that difficult. They cannot or will not face them SELVES - The God-Like part, for fear of finding out that they are not as perfect as they would like to be, and that they need to change, they **do not** like change and therefore **fear** it.

A great deal of blame must lie with religions and the

May I Know

May I know

when it is time to rest and work

also when it is time to give love and understanding.

When to refrain from giving;

to be able to receive with humbleness

and gratitude.

To know when to play innocently as a child

of the

Infinite Spirit.

churches, who wish to bind us to them, will not give us responsibility for ourselves, allowing us to dig deeper into our spiritual depth, to sort out our failings.

Reincarnation used to be in the Bible, a well known fact, until one day it was deemed that it should be taken out of the churches' teaching, for, if it was not, the churches would lose their power over the people by giving them more responsibility amongst other things.

Jesus the Christ, God, is not a building, bricks and mortar. God is truth, love, everywhere and in everyone. That is why the churches are not so full. More people are aware that priests cannot forgive sins, only God and you **yourself** can truly forgive your own sins.

Grace descends down upon people who are of great love for God, who are truly listening and practising what they preach.

These people surely ~ if grace is given by God to do so, are just as able to give blessings to a house, a person, or on a marriage.

A church is a Centre whereby people can gather and pray, this is good, but what about our homes, a prayer at night, and in the morning?

Where there is dogma, black and white ~ there God will not be or dwell.

There is good everywhere ~ this I know.

The world is in a sad state. There is no time to loose. Listen to the Masters. Listen to the God within.

Only your caring enough, your love and light ~ your prayer ~ can truly make this world a better place to live in, and save it from destruction ~ and in doing so ~ yourself reap the benefits.

So take responsibility and open up your heart

to God and the Masters.

Be PEACE MAKERS

There are many to warmonger,

to create havoc in the home and **SELF**,

More Peace Makers are needed

with sufficient understanding and love

for the whole human race.

Where are they?

Now is the time to stand up

and be counted.

Many will be your blessings,

and much light will be shed

in the world.

Turn the Other Cheek

Turn the other cheek should not be taken literally.

If someone did 'slap' our cheek, we would not wait for them to do this again willingly. This situation demands wisdom; of walking away from another attack; or better still, contemplating why this has happened ~ and can you bring peace to this situation.

It may be anger of spoken words, humiliation, whatever the reason there is no need for an attack of a physical nature.

Surely as human beings we should be above this animalistic approach? Be able to discuss, debate, or beg to differ. "Why should you?" You may ask. The answer is simple.

Any anger used by word or action against another will do harm to the one using it ~ and will return in God's time, somehow. So we cannot afford to lose our wisdom, commonsense, and behave like animals.

Most people who lose their temper, shout out, and call people names, need help in some way.

Do not try to pacify or cajole them. Try to understand the situation, the other person, and where they are coming from, then look at where *you* may have contributed to this outburst. Having done this, try to be the 'peace maker'.

If only everyone in all the world would do this, there would be no wars, no family rows, no feuding at all, and peace would reign WITHIN you and the world.

The medical profession is there to help,

not to listen to people who are full

of self pity and/or do not want

to take any responsibility

for their own welfare.

Our Relationship
With The Medical Profession

I have been asked why is it doctors, specialists and nurses all try to dominate a patient? Then again another question that comes to mind is the medical profession wonder why patients cannot take more responsibility for their own minds and bodies.

I believe there is not just one reason for these queries, but many. Above all perhaps is the pride and ego of the doctor or specialist feeling that they *should* know the answer and what to do for a patient, versus, the patient who either feels afraid to give an opinion of themselves as to what they feel may be the cause of their dis-ease; or fear that their illness causes them not to be able to explain their condition properly, so they will be misunderstood and waste the doctors time, which is fear again.

You should be able to feel security when you visit your clinic that whatever you say will be understood. That you are not treated as morons, often with irritability, but with firm truth gently given~ even if giving tablets is an easier option than this ~ this should not be so.

Likewise, you the patient need to, if possible, illness allowing, be concise in your speaking to the doctor. Allow that doctors are human beings as well as having that profession. Yes they have had training for ten years or more to become a doctor, though this should not be taken by you as an assumption that all doctors are infallible.

You/they could have had a sleepless night. You/they might have lost a loved one.

This is to point out that we are all human, can make mistakes and can have inadequacies. So why can't doctor and patient help each other in their own different ways, when they need to meet, to find a solution, in a harmonious way.

All tablets, all medicines, have side effects,

that can create further problems for you.

So, think, listen to your body

before you take anything,

the cure could lie elsewhere

with mind power, prayer, faith.

All medications have a part to play

for a while - at some time - I do believe this.

I also know mind power

and prayer are greater than any

pills or medication can ever be.

This I have proved.

Times are fast changing, patients and professionals are seeing the need to change.

It is no longer "I am the boss here" rather "lets sort out this problem together."

I do feel though that some people do rush to doctors for the slightest reason, expecting to be given pills to sort their problem out, instead of taking more responsibility for their bodies. Try to see if there is a way to help yourself before contacting the local clinic. It might be just rest you need, exercise, or change of food intake. Our bodies do try to inform us of their needs in many different ways, but, can we hear ~ are we listening? Do we want to listen? Or is it easier to get pills from the doctor, putting all the responsibility on that *one* person. This is not right.

There is much we can do to help ourselves, take responsibility for our mind and bodies.

To do this we need to go quiet within, listen to the body, to the part that is troubling you. Don't speak, just allow your intuition to guide you

Pray that you may be shown what to do for the best. It does work, and you will feel stronger by looking and thinking ~ before you leap ~ for a doctor.

Good Health ~ Bad Health

WIN or LOOSE

Good or Bad

Nice or nasty

mean or generous

Happy or unhappy

YOU

HAVE A CHOICE

IT IS YOUR DECISION

AND FROM IT

YOU BECOME

WHAT YOU ARE TODAY.

Taking Responsibility
For Our Life

No one can tell you what you *must* do, what you should say, or, harm you with what they say to you ~ unless you allow them to do so. Doctors give you tablets that you are not forced to take any more than an operation can be forced upon us.

Only you should decide, giving all situations careful thought before making your decision.

WE MUST TAKE FULL RESPONSIBILITY FOR OUR OWN MIND BODY AND SPIRIT

It is not right to expect other people to know us far better than we should know ourselves, this is simply not true, except in unusual circumstances.

You can be, and become, whatever you truly feel you can. With God and faith plus common sense, 'the sky's the limit', and so it should be.

You can ask, discuss and listen to others for advice, then use your own intuitiveness to find the solution for YOU. This is the only way to feel respect for your SELF and get the best, in any given situation, for what you need.

WE ARE RESPONSIBLE FOR OURSELVES

All have a part to play in life.

Their own path to follow.

Follow your path,

making it your very own.

♥

Do your very best

at all times,

♥

Do not flinch from disaster,

embrace it

TO BECOME STRONG

♥

JOYFUL DAYS

ARE RESTING TIMES

♥

WE NEED THEM ALL

TO GROW.

Monks, Nuns, Recluses
and Communities

Karma can make people become hermits, monks and nuns, and become recluses.

These days there are not as many 'closed' orders as there used to be. Monks and Nuns are leading a much more interactive life outside their convents and monasteries: coming to terms with life outside their boundaried walls and finding out how other people live, their needs, and just as importantly, that it is just as difficult inside their houses as it is outside, *problems come to ALL ~ EVERYWHERE.*

I wonder these days if the ways of the recluse are becoming obsolete, for, by retreating from life, we can retreat from our SELVES ~ yes, we have more time to pray and reflect, but without wisdom we also have more time to criticise and punish our minds and bodies, but what for? Do we not have enough problems, mountains to climb, without causing more difficulties for ourselves by trying to be martyrs? We do not need to marry, which gives more time for God and prayer. One can be very happy with little money, if our bodily needs are met.

Look though at the experiences that are missed to balance us out on all levels in living the life of a recluse. Marriage tries our patience, brings out any jealous and judgemental sides of our nature, makes us more understanding and giving. In return we have a human relationship for comfort and support through our life. We can help each other forward, pray together, and seeing suffering, can help those who suffer around us. We can use our money towards and for the benefit of others, as well as for our own comforts.

I have known as friends priests and so very many lovely nuns. Whilst in the human body, they are not exempt from

The only difference

between saints and sinners

is that

saints know that God is within

and act accordingly.

human suffering, but the distress and particularly frustration they can suffer, I am sure is not meant to be. There can be much overdrinking in private;guilt, if they find the opposite sex attractive. They lead an abnormal life which may be good for some but unhealthy for many.

I am not denying that some may feel chosen for this life, and be comparatively happy within it, but for many it is a 'way out' from life, or a way of life that is expected of them by their family or church.

It does not make us a more spiritual person by becoming a priest, nun or recluse.

Prayer should be an important part of *everyone's* life, and all the world can benefit from sincere prayer. Through repetition of a prayer or words said over and over again (a) we can be taken to great heights of bliss (b) we can enter a trance state (c) it can take our devotion away leaving boredom behind. We must be careful that this does not happen in closed orders, communities or otherwise.

We become better, more spiritual human beings by allowing ourselves to imbibe *all* that life has to offer, and in doing so meet it in prayer and faith. We can work through life with joy in our hearts, doing the very best we can, in any given situation. Letting ourselves grow, be changed, changing any unwanted bad habits, and slowly finding out God is within.

We are of love, peace and joy

We become at **ONE** with life.

We need never make wrong choices ~

It's ours to decide

that our choice will be the

correct one.

Unselfishness,

openmindedness,

and patience

will bring the right choice

for

that moment of time.

Making Right Choices

We are all capable of a wrong choice, unless we apply some 'golden' rules to our thinking.

It is not just a case of being black and white, we may have many options open to us.

Those who have Pure Meditation as their guide should know what to do, but for those who do not have this perfect way forward, the answer is, that we must not work with our pride and ego. Working from what is needed **not** what you **want** is vital. To find the right choice ~ think of all options. Go quietly, letting the vast computer within 'browse' through its files. If you really want the best for the situation and everyone concerned, the answer will then arrive into your consciousness.

To say a silent prayer for the correct decision is always a good start.

Do not try to force an answer ~ our minds do not take to this method.

Pray with best intentions, and faith that you will know the answer in good time. Then **accept** the answer.

This is not as easy as it sounds, especially if it is not the answer that we are looking for or wanting to hear.

Try this method ~ have faith ~ it will
work for YOU.

If we have Pure Meditation

and practise this spiritual and scientific art

with patience and perseverance,

then we can

achieve Self Realization

in one lifetime.

Karma and Repentance

We are given many chances through many life times to find our true inner self, and to find our way back to our perfection ~ to God.

Like a diamond we have many facets, each facet has to be worked on to make a whole person. Facets, or we call them lifetimes, are made up of different race experiences, gender experiences, and different personalities. Each life incorporating one or more of these. Therefore we enjoy being either woman, man, rich and poor and so on... one lifetime is not enough to perfect our being, so we are allowed as many lifetimes as is needed; be it on this earth plane or another.

When it is thought over, this system is a very fair and logical one. There must surely be a very *loving light* of knowledge to allow for our stubbornness and laziness amongst other faults which prevent us going forward to Self~Realization.

Karma means **we reap that which we sow.**

In any one of our existences, whatever we do, say or even think, will have an effect on our life and others, for example:- if you criticise and made a judgement on a person, one day, one lifetime, through someone it will 'boomerang' back to you, and you may resent it and wonder why this is happening to you.

A great deal of karma can be gathered over the years if we are not careful of what we say and do to other beings.

Once you have this knowledge, you can make sure that you do not collect any more bad karma, only good karma, for that good karma will also 'boomerang' back to you in the very same way.

And so we work our passage back home. However long it takes ~ God and the Masters are there to help you.

There is no alternative. There is a choice of how long you

Make **good** karma

Not bad.

Remember,

with Karma

you pay back to **your self**

No one else does.

This knowledge can

Set You Free

wish to take, but one day we will all be home ~ back to soul perfection. THAT IS THE SPIRITUAL LAW.

If from our hearts we are truly repentant of any bad mistake that has been made by us, then it can be taken, or melt, away from our being, though for this to happen the heart must really feel the pain of the mistake as we cry out for forgiveness.

Try not to leave this world before you ask forgiveness of others you may have harmed by a careless word or gesture, or, forgiveness to God for **more** harmful acts.

You will also need to forgive your SELF.

Karma is a **just** law. Common sense tells us that it is a good one, allowing time for us to learn this spiritual truth, and practise it well for our own benefit.

I Know

that

Love

can

move

mountains

❖

Let *us move* them together

♥

Changing the World

I am often asked if we can change the world, and if so "how?"

Yes, this is possible and in point of fact it is very necessary that we try to do so.

Each individual with their love and light holding steadfastly to peace, vibrating love, can and will help change others, who in turn will change, yet again, other people, until villages, towns, countries and last but not least ~ the world is changed into a better, more habitable place.

Individuals, groups and families, all can play an enormous part in changing the world.

For this to happen fairly quickly we need peace, wisdom and above all unconditional love in every single person. You see from this statement how difficult this beautiful and very necessary project could be.

It will happen ONE day, meanwhile, no task is too great for those who desire a better world and are willing to change themselves to be able to put this into effect.

Love begets Love

Hate begets Hate

Mother of all Creation

Infinite Beloved

Free us from all mortal desires,

for they keep us earthbound.

Free us from all

but the desire of finding Self~Realization

in this lifetime

So we may live

in the light and glory of our

Creator

Free Yourself from all Desires

The world is caught in a labyrinth of desires. It starts from babyhood and continues on through our lives until we get to an age of discretion.

Our desires and wants are always so many, ranging from 'I want more money', a bigger house, better clothes, a sports car, yacht and so our desires come to torment, perhaps, the once peaceful mind.

There is no harm in having dreams of what we would like, as long as we do not let our dreams and desires become our MASTER. They must not be allowed to become of primary importance ~ if they are allowed to do so, then, the mental suffering begins by making us discontented, frustrated and un-happy in our everyday life.

I hope that you are wise enough to know your own *needs*, though wants and desires we need to be completely free of.

There is a system taught whereby people are shown how to use their mind power to win the lottery, get a better job and so on.... what a waste of our energy, when all we have to do to receive what we need, is to look for God first within, be a loving peaceful wise human being, and by being and giving like this, you will attract the positive good *needs* to yourself. Otherwise a situation is created whereby you get more than you want or bargain for, upsetting the 'would be' natural balance of your life, unless of course you need an imbalance at that time of your life ~ because ~ you may need it to progress spiritually ~ as well as in the mortal sense.

There is a right time and place for all the major happenings in your life, you need to be aware when these events and hap-penings are there for you to take advantage of. This is not mean-ing to say that you do not need to do some work yourself.

All things NEEDED

Come to those that wait with faith

If you push too hard,

and the door keeps closed,

beware, have patience,

pray, and know that

with the combined effort

of your SELF, God and Guru

all will be given to you

of your needs ~ even more so

if you wait for the right time and place

Then it **will** happen

Knock, and if the door does not open, do not push it too hard, for it has to close before a better one can open.

You can cause a postponement of something happening by the negative energy of 'demanding'

A simple illustration is:– how often people say to me 'I have no girl/boyfriend ~ I keep asking and looking'. STOP doing this and suddenly ~ right time and place ~ they are there ~ the partner that you have needed.

Desires work from the lower plane of energy, solar plexus, emotional level.

State your needs in prayer then live for the moment in life ~ that soon passes.

Free yourself of ALL desires, and you will feel a freedom that you have never known before.

Pure Meditation

is my spiritual food.

May I feed deeper and longer in Your Presence.

Give me my daily bread,

so that I may feed others

with the food

of peace, light and love.

Physical and Spiritual Food

When we were perfected and only of light we did not need to eat mortal food. We had the spiritual food of the heavens.

First and foremost whilst in the body, we still need our spiritual food which is Pure Meditation and prayer. We need also to give to others some of this spiritual food, which in itself is Divine energy and if we do this in our way with love and healing, within our family or outside it, then we do not get what I call 'spiritual indigestion' (free flow of energy is restricted by 'hoarding' it in our body.)

All is energy and energy must be free~flowing or it can do harm. While having a mortal body and putting it to work most days, the body will need its' nourishment. It would be unwise and ridiculous to say that it needs nothing, but we should be careful what food is put into the body.

The food should be of good quality. Not too much, and it should cater for a particular body's needs, for everyone, some foods may have to be subtracted. Why not? Each body is special.

As a person grows in the spiritual way, their intake of food will become less, not so much mortal food is needed. Their tastes for different foods will change. The taste buds become more refined so that they do not wish to smother everything in tomato ketchup and other such sauces, their preference being for blander type foods ~ with a more natural flavour.

More often than not the person does not give certain foods like beef, lamb and chicken up. It ~ the food ~ gives *them* up ~ they are unable to 'stomach it' any longer.

I am not a great believer in diets. I find people who have small amounts of good food with plenty of the spiritual food are slimmer, (as opposed to thin) much healthier and younger looking.

That can't be a bad thing.

Give the body its due

No more than that, for the

body can be greedy, taking up

all of your time, so there

is no time left for

your much needed

spiritual food.

Without this food ~

you will *exist*

not *live*

It is a known fact today that Junk Food is causing obesity in many people alongside the bad habit of overeating.

For whatever reason a person 'over indulges' it does not make it right to do so, as our body is a vessel lent to us (we did not make it ourselves) to house the Christ power and Holy Spirit.

You can cultivate bad eating habits or good eating habits ~ it is up to you ~ though if you want a healthy mind and body, then cultivating good habits, and keeping to them, is the obvious answer.

Food is there for us to use *wisely*.

NOT

for *food* to use us *unwisely*.

❣

Do not try to dissect **bad**,

to find a reason for everything.

Accept there is a *reason*

and go along in this faith.

So, as you grow in wisdom,

will you realise the truth,

and not before.

~

Reasons can be very much in

evidence *or* extremely subtle

~

You will not find the depth of reason from intellect,

but only from a purity of thought,

breadth of understanding

and spiritual awareness

Is there a Reason for Everything in Life?

Yes, there is a reason for everything and everyone, even every happening in life.

What is the point of *anything* if there is not a reason and an outcome for it?

Nature is there to feed us, bring us comfort, to enjoy. Houses are to give us sanctuary from the elements, a home, comfort. Human beings are there for us as friends, advice-givers, companions and helpers ~ to help us on our path of life. Equally, they bring problems which test us in patience and fortitude, giving us a chance to have a listening ear, *develop* our patience, and to become stronger individuals from these encounters.

A thought, an act, has a reason, if we see and can allow it to be shown to us. Common sense and logic denotes that there is a reason for everything.

Often there has been cause for me to verbally demonstrate this to a person. No one has ever asked me anything on this subject that has not enabled me to show a very good reason for life and everything in it, in people and for all circumstances.

Intellectuals can debate this and think up a man~made answer to explain this. It will not hold water.

I have long ago tried to find disbelief

only to find BELIEF.

There is but One Pure Energy.

God ~ Master souls of light and love

know of these dangers, and such words

written to this effect are in the Bible.

✦

First seek the kingdom of God within,

of peace, love, wisdom,

and knowledge ~ to make you God~like

❖

When you need to feel, hear, know or see,

so will it happen, but with great

depth of spirituality and a touch of deep knowing.

Then no harm will be done

to your mind, body or spirit.

✦

OTHERWISE DO NOT DELVE

INTO

Things you do not understand.

Are Mediumship and Clairvoyance Needed Now?

Well there are some people who will always think they need to know the future, or what has happened in the past. There is a dangerously inquisitive interest in such matters that are truthfully best left well alone, but human nature being what it is, I doubt that this will happen for many a year until people have more knowledge of the difference between *psychic* and *spiritual*.

We all have the ability to feel, see and hear. If we want to tune into a psychic wavelength, then with tuition, it is possible to do so, but, you do *need* to realize that you are tuning into lower planes with souls on these lower vibrations (or energy levels) so information will not always be accurate because of **their** level, and often information given can be very dangerous because of this. Much depends on the medium who may be a lovely person, but, it will still not be the higher planes that they are contacting. Also, if we need to be contacted by those souls passed over, it would happen naturally to us without a medium.

I believe for whatever reason, psychic powers may have been needed in years gone by;

they are not needed now

and should not be used any longer

for we have our own spiritual insight, our own abilities of intuition, our own common sense. All these attributes will show or give us any information that we may need to help us with any given personal event or problem.

No worthwhile book

like the Bible, Koran or Bhagavad Gita

can be read and understood fully on the first reading.

No Master or person of great spiritual depth

will be understood straight away, for,

the way they speak

and the words with which they speak

may have a foreign, spiritual, intonation to them

that you do not completely comprehend.

You need to listen carefully,

digest and always come back for more

to expand the thinking capacity

of your mind.

We Think
at the Level that We Are

My dear ones, you need patience and tolerance with every-one you meet and speak to, for each and every one person will be at a different level of thinking using their own experiences as a 'yard stick'.

You cannot expect them to understand fully your words or your deeds, that is unless you explain them fully, and even then the depth of their understanding may not be one hundred per-cent. Why? because very few minds are wide enough in breadth and vision to take on a saying or idea that is foreign to them, so, they can only understand to the level that they are at, at that one given time. Misunderstandings come when you expect more of them than they are able to understand.

That is why I find it pays to spend as long a time as is neces-sary explaining a point or a reason why *fully*, so a person can receive the fuller depth of what I am saying ~ I call it 'doing the A to Z'. Even then, we cannot expect them to fully understand, feel our depth and see our minds.

When we read a good book of depth we can always re~read to find more of interest in it. So it is with people and minds.

Small minds think alike

Great minds think alike

SO IT IS.

"Give us Peace
Let us feel love in our hearts
for all creation"

Mata Yogananda Mahasaya Dharma

Main house of the Self Realization Meditation Healing Centre, Somerset, UK.

Mata Yogananda
Mahasaya Dharma
with Devotees
at Satsanga,
Mother Centre,
England, 2002

The True Seeing Eye

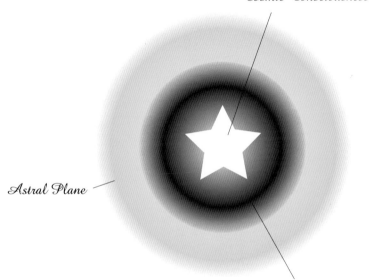

Cosmic Consciousness

Astral Plane

Causal Plane

The Eye of Delight

With our two eyes we see the world. But our *third* eye situated in the middle brow, is the one that sees the most.

When we have Pure Meditation and practise with devotion, with perseverance and dedication, then our whole life changes for the better. Spiritually, we grow, and with the 'Crown Jewel' of Pure Meditation you realise that you need never feel alone again. Life with all its problems seems much easier to deal with. Your ego and pride you see, at last, to deal with, making life fuller and sweeter for our living.

We look to giving of our thanks and love ∼ we receive many blessings. Do not look for psychic happenings, beware of these, do not allow them, but focus rather on all that is of a spiritual dimension, for one day you will feel the joy, love and bliss that you seek.

The *third* eye is of light ∼ the seeing eye. Sometimes, without want, you can see the most beautiful colours, sometimes you may see rings of gold and blue with a five pointed star within.

These things we see ∼ on our progress when least expected. Enjoy the vision. Do not try to hold on to it ∼ for by doing so it will melt away sooner. Just give a thank-you for the gift. House it in your heart but do not dwell on it, for it is but one of many gifts to come your way through Pure Meditation.

Be still and listen
to the voice and sound of all creation.
For in Creation there are many wonderous sounds to be heard.

The wind caressing the trees,
The trees dancing to its rhythm,
leaves rustling,
birds, each singing their own song of life.

While flowers nod their heads
beckoning you to them,
to look and see the variation of colours
they provide us with.

We have only to be still within
to receive from life
of its beauty, joy and energies.

Go hug a tree
and receive

Verbal Fasting

We all speak too much with chatter, gossip or even within good intelligent conversation. There are many reasons why this takes place. Perhaps we are not used to being vocally silent and feel threatened by it. It could be we are 'chatterboxes', vocal without thought, or perhaps sadly we feel lonely or unheard, a nobody, without speech and need an ear to air our views.

Whatever the reason is, we need to think about our need to vocalise. We need to remember that each time we speak we are using a certain amount of energy, and though speech may have to continue for quite a while, nevertheless, it can 'drain' our energies.

There is another important factor to take into account, and that is, we cannot hear our *intuition* clearly if we are talking, yes we may hear our ego, pride and common sense but not our high *intuitive wisdom*. We cannot hear God.

We need to have a verbal fast at least for part of each day and for one whole day if possible, not only to give our voice and vocal chords a good rest, but also to allow any further spiritual or creative thoughts to descend upon us.

One mealtime held in silence, means that we can value and masticate our food leading to a better digestion ~ and peace at the table. This is also a good habit for children to form. There are many good reasons for cultivating such a worthwhile habit of a verbal fast.

Our hearing is taken for granted.

So precious is it,

yet we treat it with disdain, carelessly.

⟫═┼═⟪

Many people are partially or fully deaf

and though compensation takes place

with their other faculties being more fully awoken,

they know the blessing of being able to hear.

✳

Treat your hearing with respect,

so it lasts you for your whole life span.

┼═⟫═⟪═┼

Fasting from Sound

Our ears are taking in sounds all the time that we are awake. From the radio, television, telephone, while out at work and shopping. These are the sounds we know of in our conscious mind and we are used to allowing these sounds in, but, what about the sounds that we do not hear so easily? The electromagnetic vibratory sounds, ones that are subtle, less intrusive to our conscious mind, though impinging just the same without our realization of them doing so. To be aware of these facts is important, still more important is what you do about it.

Young people these days seem to like loud music whenever it is being played. They do not realize what harm it is doing to their eardrums, the effect it could have on them later in their lifetime. Continuous loud sounds can and often do distort the hearing so that gentle sounds in nature and of people talking quietly may not be heard.

Our hearing is very precious and we should treat it with the respect it deserves.

Sometimes it is beneficial to cut out all sounds and rest in silence with only the sounds of nature around us.

Children should be brought up with this knowledge, starting from a very early age.

This is not necessarily easy to do, though well worthwhile imparting in speech and action, ensuring that they do not suffer any deafness of any kind later on in their life.

Master your Self

Master your body

Get to know its *needs.*

It is your vessel, for life,

housing the Christ Power

the Holy Spirit.

Look after it well,

so it looks after you

Giving you service

for as long as you need it.

Fasting

I do not believe in treating the body harshly in any way, and I do put fasting in that category. Even on the spiritual path it does not help us, by fasting heavily.

If on the spiritual path we need less intake of food, we shall feel a need to reduce our intake intuitively. Otherwise we open ourselves up to the wrong sort of 'intake' for the body and mind.

It is highly probable that people who make a habit of over-indulging themselves with food will not wish to acknowledge the 'inner voice' telling them to cut down their food intake. They do not realise how coarse their taste buds have become.

To eat less, or reduce the food level of intake into the body when we eat too much, of course, is worthwhile. The kind of food we eat is important to our health and wellbeing. This should always be done by your inner feeling (gut feeling) of what is needed for you ~ your body.

There are less nutrients in the earth now, so, we could lack some vital minerals from time to time, vitamins and other such supplements. Once again, be careful, use your discretion ~ your intuition ~ that will give you that strong feeling of which supple-ments your body is in need of at that moment of time, and also when it could do with a break from them.

My body tells me through intuition what it needs ~ and when.

Learn this art and it will do the same for you.

God works through YOUR body

Sleepless Nights

We cannot always sleep straight away on our retiring to bed. The hours that we do sleep are not always of the same duration. So the sleep state is different on many counts, including how much sleep we actually need.

For retiring to bed ~ and to sleep, we need to prepare ourselves for the occasion. Try not to watch violent films beforehand. No arguments left to cause disruption. Do not overeat - no coffee or strong tea (stimulants.)

a) Sit in a Meditative State to set the scene.

b) Take a walk before sleep.

c) Make sure you have a well-aired room.

d) Perhaps read a book, or listen to the radio.

It is your decision for everyone is different on different nights.

One way *not* to sleep is to worry about sleeping and how many hours you *think* you *have* to get to be mobile the next day. Do remember it isn't the *quantity* but the *quality* of the sleep state that counts.

If sleep evades you, move ~ get up; make yourself a drink; Meditate; write a letter; read; do some ironing and soon you will feel tired enough to return to your bed. Do so, without concern, having enjoyed your time up ~ it has been productive, and you will find sleep will come ~ with quality.

Too many people toss and turn, staying in their bed demanding sleep. This never works.

Be gentle and loving towards yourself as you would be to a child that cannot sleep. You would talk to them, cuddle them, give them a warm drink, and then put them back to bed. Do the same with yourself. We very rarely need as much sleep as we think we do, in fact we can make do with very little sleep if needs be, without any harm being done ~ **providing** we do not worry and get concerned over the thought of *less sleep.*

Anything we do ~ to gain benefit from
needs thought and preparation.

Peaceful spiritual thoughts

Lead to a Restful, good night's sleep.

A Place of Rest

When we finish our work on this earth plane

⁂

There is a place of rest,

of peace, where we shall know

no pain.

We shall be free of worry

of the passing of time.

No burden shall be ours

only rest and peace for

as long as we need.

⁂

Prepare to Pass in Peace ~ Joy

Passing should be seen and spoken about not as a sad terrible way to 'go on' but in light of the expectation of another life, a better one that we shall be leaving this world to pass into.

The day that we are born we are already on our way to this great event.

'We are born to die.'

As this is one of the greater events of our lifetime, should we not treat it as so by acknowledging it is going to happen, at some time, some place, somewhere, and then when it feels the right time in our life to do so, prepare ~ not with haste if this is possible, but slowly and peacefully. Making a Will. Putting our house in order, so that we are aware all has been done for the occasion.

Still people have a fear of passing, lacking the much needed knowledge that we do not need to end our life frustrated, with worry, in fear and not knowing that there *is* another life ahead of them.

Jesus told us there was another life to go to, saying, 'For in my Father's House there are many mansions' which means, where we go depends on the life that we live here on this earth plane.

Do not let friends and family grieve for us for too long. A short period of grief will help them come to terms with your passing. Too much grief over a long period of time will *not* help **you** to rest and as quickly as possible adjust to your new life and home. Tell them of this, explain how you feel well beforehand.

If there is love between you both, then you will be able to meet again later on, meanwhile, a link of love is never broken, and it is amazing how you will be able to help them (God willing) from your new home.

Creator of all Creation

help me to know WHEN

I have completed my work here.

Help me to hear the call

from you ~my Creator.

May my journey be swift into the light

of your love,

where I may once again do Thy Will.

SO BE IT.

When it is time to pack your 'bag' you need only a small bag of peace, faith and surrender to the knowledge that it's YOUR time. Keep as quiet as you can, enjoy others company, but not so much that you get overtired, for you have a very important journey to make. Partake in soft music, spiritual book-reading if you wish, though try to relax into a contemplative state. You will sleep more ~ do so, eat less, that is good ~ 'You can't travel *light* on a full stomach'

Make certain that you have money put by for a ceremony, a Will made, as mentioned before, so that there is no disharmony, and anything else you can think of that paves the way to an easier dealing of matters by all concerned, and thereby releasing your mind to deal with more important issues.

It is so very important ~ *how* we pass ~ as to what happens when we do.

So smile ~ God awaits you.

Infinite Beloved,

may my conscience be my guide

in all that I do and say.

Help me to hear clearly

and not turn a deaf ear.

Do not allow ego or pride

to be the stronger force.

Guide me to all that I need to know.

Let Your Conscience
Be Your Guide

You have a very finely tuned faculty called a conscience. The more that you use this faculty the more finely tuned it becomes. It is within you as a safeguard against wrong speech, bad behaviour. It has many useful reasons for being with you.

Conscience is aligned to intuition in that our conscience gives us a TAP on the shoulder if we are straying from our path. If we are aware of the TAP and stop, intuition will come in and help to guide you onto the 'right track', the best way to proceed.

Your wants and stubbornness can override the conscience very easily, pretending that you have not heard. Do not do this for it is at your own peril if you do.

Your conscience helps you to be a better person, more thoughtful and giving to others, be less judgemental and more humble.

Let it guide you.

Concentration can bring us

success in all that we do.

It makes it easier

to find the God within.

Light of my heart and EYE

help me to have the power of concentration,

so that all my acts are perfected,

and my words

always of the highest wisdom.

That my listening ear will hear

accurately and clearly what others say to me

thus showing respect for ALL OF LIFE.

The Importance of Concentration

I find few people have very good powers of concentration. This lack can cause many problems for them including accidents.

Learning to concentrate fully, one hundred percent on the small things in our life, will help us when the bigger issues come along, for then, without our full concentration the solving of them may be very difficult.

Whilst concentrating on any one given topic, we should be oblivious to all else. So, if someone is relating an incident to us, we should be with them one hundred percent ~ few people do this, even though they are often not aware that they are *not* doing so.

With family, at work, the same concentration should be applied. It shows respect for the person and for what is being said, making sure that we know and retain what is being said to us in the workplace, or that our work is being done to the best that we can possibly (humanly) do it.

If you do not have this ability, it can be learnt. You can teach yourself by continual practise of concentrating whenever you do *anything*. Once you have this ability, it is yours for life. Do this before you have children, for then it is nigh on impossible, as you will be doing several things at once for quite a few years to come.

The Truth Mirror

Look in the mirror
See if you look content,
or does the face droop?

Smile at your image.
See the difference it makes
not only to your face
but to how you feel inside yourself.

Practise a smile ~
a congenial look ~
and practise
your sense of humour.

your sense of humour.
and practise
a congenial look ~
Practise a smile ~

but to how you feel inside yourself.
not only to your face
See the difference it makes
Smile at your image.

or does the face droop?
See if you look content,
Look in the mirror

Let's Keep Our Sense of Humour

My dear one, a sense of humour is so very important.

If when you do something silly, you can smile or laugh at yourself, it takes the sting out of the incident and makes you feel more relaxed and balanced.

Likewise, if we can find a sense of humour shining through a problem, the problem will seem less 'heavy' and more surmountable. It is also a tonic, a comforter and a conciliatory aid.

Life could be very dull for those without one, I myself would not like to be without one or to live with people who could not see the funny side of life ~ or themselves.

What a tonic it is to those who can have an extension of humour ~ which is a good laugh.

It has been proved only recently (though it is also commonsense) that a *good laugh* makes people happier, becoming healthier with possibly a longer lifespan. Well, either way, humour and laughter are good for us all ~ and for you.

Let your humour show itself.

☺

On a more spiritual note,

holding problems, worries inside,

the stress factor,

are all known that they can and do

contribute to colon problems.

Do think on this,

see if you are harbouring

any worries and fears.

Deal with them *NOW.*

All parts of our body are connected

to each other to a greater or lesser degree.

Develop your faith

for with faith ~ you will have no fear.

Knowledge of a Dis-ease: Constipation

I do not believe that constipation is taken seriously enough. Its effects can be horrendous if experienced over a long period of time without doing anything about it.

Taking corrective tablets and medicines is not the answer. They can do more harm than good depending on the cause. Straining while having a bowel movement can cause further long~term problems. Waste material which clogs, blocks and cannot be evacuated, will turn into a substance that could poison the whole system.

It is not always how often we go that counts so much as how we perform, for example ~ do you give yourself time, time for this act ~ to complete the job? No straining ~ and with your mind on what you are doing? All very important points to look at. Do not be squeamish, check if the evacuation has been a good one, even its' colour is important. One of my patients was con-cerned because his stools passed were of a red colour. I asked him what he had been eating, amongst other things. His reply was 'beetroot'. Need I say more!

Good wholesome food is needed. No overeating. Exercise and a good intake of fluid usually keeps movement. Gentle efflourage can help. If not, try to work out what you need to do to put things right. If you can not of course, see a doctor.

Harsh toilet paper does not help. For women they should always wipe from front to back for hygiene purposes.

To encourage a Good Habit regular times need to be kept for such matters ~ the body remembers what and when it usually performs. Don't make things complicated for its' remembrance.

I have only been able to gloss over this important subject as there are many reasons for this dis~ease.

All I ask is that you do not take this condition too lightly.

Other Thoughts

Masturbation is deemed wrong because

it excites ~ with unnatural actions ~

our bodies lower energy centres,

thus causing the need of satisfaction

with release and dissipation of those

energies that can otherwise

be harnessed and put to good use.

♥

Repetition of such action

over a long period of time

can not only make the body listless

but also can drain our sexual energy so

that it can affect a permanent relationship.

Note that there is a means of raising and changing this energy,

so that it is not lost by our bodies.

It is taught in the intensive course of Pure Meditation.

Homosexuality

I am using the word 'gay' here to mean both male and female gay, or homosexual, people.

A lack of knowledge in this subject still abounds, particularly of the spiritual dimension.

How do people find out that they are gay, or, think they are?

We all know experimentation starts at a very early age for both sexes, firstly, wonderment at our own bodies, from then on its a known fact that a certain amount of masturbation takes place in many cases. We then have colleges, which may be all boy or all girl, which gives ample opportunity for crushes, experimentation and 'coupling'. Many go on from here to lead heterosexual lives ~ some do not.

Other instances that can lead to a person becoming gay are: being raped when young; being badly treated by the opposite sex; a boy dressed up from birth as a girl and treated like one ~ who could then behave abnormally in adult life to become a transvestite; these are all possibilities.

I have had dealings with many gay people. They are like most people, in the main very lovely and open hearted. Some that I have known have changed their mind about themselves, married, and are content with their life.

We should be able to feel love for male and female without necessarily making it a sexual relationship.

It is a spiritual law that we should 'love each other as we love ourselves'. Whether we allow it to become physical and sexual is up to each individual ~ most of the time, except in situations where the taking of drugs, and rape, are concerned.

The spiritual side of the issue of homosexuality is that we are here on this earth plane to find our true self, balance our yin and yang energies. Whereas men are more down-to-earth creatures, women are more emotional, one difference that can be used to explain a point.

Men need to have more balanced female energies in them, whereas women need more of the male energy. So if one *is* or *becomes* gay, this upsets the inner balance both emotionally and

A Prayer for All

God who loves all,

help us to a purer mind,

a peaceful mind and body.

May we give and receive love

in its' purest state

May we befriend and

be befriended

Help us to find the balance

of our energies.

Leading us

to Self~Realization

in other ways even more, making it much harder to balance oneself, and to find Self~Realization in this lifetime because of these facts. *It can be done,* though very rarely, because of the inner conflict and emotions ~ which are not evenly balanced.

Man can feel great affection for another man. Likewise woman with woman.

We need to remember that we can love many attributes of a person, make them a friend or partner without bringing *sexual* energy/involvement into that love.

* Why make man and woman if we only needed ONE sex?

* We could all be gay if we let ourselves be.

I wonder how much of this is hormonal as opposed to a set of circumstances paving the way!

Bearing in mind that we all have a balance of hormones within our bodies and that some take predominance over others, making us male or female, it stands to reason I believe that as we are born as one sex ~ I personally do not believe we should change it ~ for it is with us for a reason.

If a person as a man can father several children and then decide he feels more a woman and changes his role into that of a woman, where does it leave karma and the soul that is born?

We have to find our true self which is **both** male and female ~ for we maintain the essence of both within us all our lives ~ the energies need to be balanced perfectly ~ to go forward to a *perfect state*.

The body's message can be so strong that it can overrule the mind and make life unbearable unless we allow a change to take place.

I would query how many people find perfect peace by doing so, and with full spiritual knowledge of its' effects on our mind, body and spirit , would they rethink before taking such extreme measures?

We should face this truth with love for all. No criticism or judgement should ever be within our hearts or minds ~ for it is not in mine as I write these words.

169

Life is precious

Life is good

Whatever it may bring

open your *eye*

open your Mind

and let your heart sing.

For God is within

You

What Right Have We
to Take A Life

We do not even own our own life. It is committing a
murder, whichever way one tries to make justification with
excuses, in **taking** one.

Keeping a person alive with mechanical aids is *not* normal
living. There is no true living in such a state and we were never
meant to prolong our lifespan like that.

I can understand that we wish to keep our loved ones here in
their body for as long as it is humanly possible, but, is not **quality
of life more important than quantity?**

Every one body/soul has a natural life span, whether we pass
of old age or of a dis-ease. The most important thing is to live life
well, making the most of each day.

When we are ill we try to find ways of getting better, and
that is how it should be. Though there will come a time when
our loved ones and ourself will have fulfilled our spiritual work ~
finished our 'life span', and then when that time comes it needs to
happen naturally, for only God knows, if, through pain at the end
of our life we still may be working out our last bit of karma,
releasing our *self* so we may never have to pass this way again.

Only your higher self~soul~God knows what is needed,
and it is the most important time at the end of a life span to get it
right.

With or without pain there may be karma to work out, we
need to therefore stay alive naturally till God calls and our spirit
soul gets restless to leave the body ~ then start 'packing our bag'
for the journey into our next life.

If we take another's life (except in self defence, or defending
others) then we could do harm to them ~ spiritually ~ and to
ourselves.

My God,

I need help

to feel the presence of your peace and love.

To overcome this desperate

feeling of being unwanted, lost

that nothing is for me.

You know of my feelings

you know of my thoughts.

Grant me peace

So that I may see the

light of wisdom.

If we commit suicide, we are taking our own life which is *not* ours to take.

We come back on this earth plane to work through our karma, we **need** to do this. We knew before we were born that we wanted to ~ and were going to, so, this must be *allowed* to be done.

Taking a life - however difficult it is for the person, is murder and taking our own life is also murder of our SELF making life more difficult for ourselves ~ for we shall have then to pass this way again.

I understand how difficult it can be.

But this is the truth that

needs to be written.

A Request

Infinite Beloved help me

in my quest for freedom

from jealousy.

With the knowledge that it

does untold harm to my SELF and others,

I pray for the wisdom and strength

to free myself from this bondage.

Please ~ help me

Jealousy

Jealousy need not remain in a persons make-up, if, from a very early age the parents are wise enough to show their children how to share the toys, presents, and their affection, coupled with words of wisdom later on, as they reach an age of true under-standing.

If you have a jealous nature, beware, for it can totally ruin your life and others' lives.

They say there cannot be love without having a modicum of jealousy. This may be so, though it is still for the best if all jealousy can be eradicated, for, one has to let others have freedom of decision–making whatever the outcome.

1. Don't try to 'cage' people, else they may 'fly' away.
2. Possessions, a house, a person are not ours to posess.
   They could disappear in a 'flash'.
3. So why be jealous of other people and their possessions, or a person needing more freedom?

Whatever the reason, use **commonsense** and **wisdom** to dispel this unwanted trait. **Pray** for strength to do so.

These three going hand in hand will help you see the folly of such feelings and how to disperse them.

SET YOURSELF FREE

Do not wander too far

in your travels to God Realization.

There are many small paths

that can seem more ideal,

that if walked upon will take you

off this True Path.

⸻

Others will try with false

promises, with more aplomb and glitter.

Refrain, do not gaze too long.

Keep faithfully to your pathway

of Pure Meditation ∼ peace ∼ truth ∼ love.

And you will reap

all you need from your seven chakras.

Chakras
~ how many are there?

I never care for black and white statements, for there are always 'greys' inbetween, so when someone asks this question, which has happened quite often, I usually will ask them a question to start with, it being "do you need to know, does it matter?"

I'm a great believer that we get to *know* ~ what we need to *know* ~ when we need to *know* whatever it is.

Having said that ~ I rest my case and say:-
The body has many energy ~ chakra points which are used in acupuncture or can be used in acupressure by a said therapist ~ and also by ourselves in healing if we work with our intuition.

There are seven major Chakra points in the body, some people say more, personally I feel that these seven points are all we need to know about for our spiritual progress to Self Realization, that is unless you are an acupuncturist or a therapist in some other form of body enhancement.

If it is your spiritual advancement that you care most about then the seven chakras within your Pure Meditation practise are all that you really need to know about and USE.

Go with God

Find the God within first,

above all else, and *all*

shall be added unto you.

I hope that I have common sense and intelligence ~

intellect ~ I doubt.

I went to God first and I found

from my experience that

all else *is added to you* ~

that is needed for this lifetime.

Every thing in every way.

Intellect

Common sense, intelligence, intellect.
Most people have one or two of these attributes, very rarely all three.

We certainly need common sense, it is useful to be intelligent, if we have intellect alongside the other two, then we are very fortunate indeed, though intellect does have its 'downside' when it comes to the spiritual path.

Intellect likes to dissect everything, debate, discuss around and about the topic in question. It does not have faith as a component. If eventually finding faith, it can be easily shaken because of the intellect's ability to want to keep on dissecting in the mind.

Commonsense and/or intelligence can accept more readily.

Over the many years of teaching I have found this to be in the main true; of course, there are always exceptions.

If those wishing to find Self~Realization can put the intellect on one side whilst dealing with spiritual truths and the truth of themselves, then, after finding their *true* spirituality, it would be safe and beneficial to bring their intellect back into use again.

However **intuition** and **faith** will make up for any one that we may lack.

Our brain ~ that vast 'computer' ~ houses our intellect.

When is intellect to be used?

When is it **not** not to be used?

That is the question.

The answer is when we have found the *WISDOM* **when** to use it.

Acknowledgement and Prayer

Respect sets us free

from rudeness and bad manners.

Respect gives to us our own self~respect.

Quality means we wish for the best

in every way

and will be concentrating fully.

These

are spiritual qualities

which are needed for Self Realization.

Infinite Beloved

Help me to have quality and respect

for all of life ~ so that I may

become more Godlike.

Quality and Respect for Life

Many people complain that their lifespan is not long enough to fulfil all that they need to do and perfect. My answer, in truth, is, if you do not *squander* time you will be given all the time that you require.

Though more important than quantity is quality. If you have a holiday with quantity but not of quality ~ of what use is it to you? Or if our work is done with plenty of time to do it in, but suppose it is not of quality? What use is it?

Quality must always be put ahead of quantity in everything, only then can you feel true respect for your endeavours and yourself.

Respect for all of life ~ all peoples ~ all that you do ~ and with what you say. All these are sadly lacking in the life of today. It does not have to be so with you.

Always go for quality first and foremost. Add respect to all that you think, say and do and your blessings will be many.

For giving quality and respect is giving of Love.

Infinite Beloved

I wish to rely on my inner wisdom,

my truth.

Help me to solve all problems

myself ~ with the Divine Power that lives within me.

To Master my mind, body,

and emotional Self,

so truth and wisdom will for ever

guide my footsteps.

Aum

Relying On Your Self

The Infinite Beloved has given to us great powers to reason with, to be master of our selves and all we survey.

It is important that you learn how to rely on your self and your intuitive wisdom because no other person can truly know what you are thinking, feeling, and the 'whys' of what you do, except *you* your *SELF*.

Relying on others can bring its' disappointments and dangers. God gave you a mind to use, use it.

Other people can be a 'sounding board' for you, whom you can talk and listen to. Still you have to make THE decision, rely on your own common sense and wisdom.

This not only helps you become more self-reliant but stronger in every way, for your path is your very own, no—one else's. What is good for others may not be good for you.

Do not doubt your ability, or else you doubt the ability of the Holy Spirit within ~ to help and guide you.

Have faith in YOUR *SELF.*

PRACTICE MAKES PERFECT.

A Prayer

I pray for the world,

and all peoples,

that this great cleansing taking place

will lead the way

to complete peace and harmony

between nations,

and between all races and religions.

May the world be as ONE

and

the Divine Power reign supreme

in all

Om

Tragedies and Disasters

These words to most people sound very unpleasant, though, if it is looked at through a different perspective ~ in the spiritual dimension ~ then we can see there is another side to these words.

In tragedies and disasters, be it wars, volcanic eruptions, rape or shootings, karma is being worked out.

Countries have their own kind of karma, as, do human beings. A country can slowly build its' own karma, while humans can bring theirs over from a past life as well as creating more karma in this life time.

It is a just Spiritual Law

'What we Sow we Reap'

If someone has killed another person/soul in a lifetime, then, likewise, they may be on the receiving end in another, thus, their karma is being worked out.

With a country, if it makes a war against another, unless under extreme provocation, then that country will also be warred upon. The people involved will know (their soul will) of what will happen to them ~ before they are born. Though they will choose to work their karma out now, in this way, during a war or whatever way it may be best for them, it will be obliterated from their conscious mind on birth, so they will not bear the burden of this knowledge.

When the time comes they will receive help while the karma is being worked out, by their higher consciousness.

So therefore all seemingly horrific happenings are brought about by the countries and/or human beings themselves, and as such, there always is a payback time. A cleansing takes place, thereby good will eventually come from such happenings.

Oh! Infinite Beloved

Help us in this dark passage of time

Shed the light

so

it illuminates our path

to peace

Throughout the world

If someone harms another or steals another person's belongings, providing the person who has stolen gives the said thing back and makes a *heartf*elt apology, or, in case of harming another with lies and gossip, the person regrets their actions apologises from the heart, then, that person will be cleared of **that** karmic act, and it will not have to come back to them ~ to clear.
I repeat ~ it must be heartfelt and deeply sincere for this to happen.

That is why I pray that each and every person thinks well before they say or do something to another person that will incur karma.

Be not judgemental, or criticise others. Be of love, peace, wisdom, so the karma will burn itself out ~

by your unconditional love

and worthy humble acts to all other souls of God.

Dear God,

♥

As I come before you,

I seek the arms of love

and the joy of rebirth

of my soul and spirit.

Guide me to the light,

forgive me my sins,

so I may imbibe in your loving light always

A devotee

What Happens When We Pass?

There has been much debate on this subject with some people telling of their experiences when their heart stopped beating for a while, under anaesthetic, and also stories from beyond the grave.

My belief is that when our spirit leaves the body, we have time to adjust to the realization of still being alive elsewhere.

That we do see our *whole* life, like a ciné film, rolling before us, allowing us to see very quickly the progress or NON– progress that we have made. There is no time in spirit, so it cannot be categorised, sufficient to say we are met and guided forward to where we need to be, and belong, to help further our progress.

We may need to rest awhile before this happens, but, eventually we shall be with spirit/people of like minds for there are many different planes~levels in the kingdom of the Infinite Beloved.

Have no fear, for you shall be well taken care of. For truth, honesty, peace, joy and unconditional love reign supreme in the heavens, and by your deeds shall you be known.

Sit quietly

and Meditate

~ ask that your

path will be shown to you.

~

That your talents will be shown

to be made full use of

for the good of all;

and,

though memories of a talent may be felt,

that we may see

it as such, and not for this

lifetime

and so

fulfil our destiny to perfection.

Exceptional Talents

You all have talents within, some more in evidence than others, which may have to be found and resurrected.

Here we are speaking of prodigies, very young people who can draw, sing, dance or play an instrument (if not several) at an extremely early age. To have the capability of doing any of these arts so well, so young, means that they would have brought this level of attainment over from another lifetime, probably their last lifetime, when there will be an 'unfinished' feeling from that life, with that particular form or art.

Some 'pass on' at an early age having accomplished their *need* and fulfilment of their part in life, others go on to further the ART for all to benefit from. There can never be any black and white in spiritual life, there are always many more reasons.

That only our 'higher self' truly knows.

If we have a leaning towards one particular art form, no doubt it will be a memory from the past. What we do with that memory depends on us. We can carry on with it or find another talent and forward that one ~ instead.

The sky is the limit if we have faith in ourselves as souls of the one universal God.

Sweet Jesus,

Great Master Soul.

✝

Help me not to doubt people

Not to mistrust good intentions

☀

Help me to show

understanding and wisdom,

to see the depth in all

people and in all events.

☦

If I cannot do this, then help

me to accept there is a reason

without my full comprehension,

so that I may grow in spirit

and harm none with my thoughts.

Doubt
Can Destroy
Your Faith and Yourself

Doubt can creep in by a chance remark from someone or because we are tired and low in our energies, or through not being able to understand fully a topic of conversation or an event.

Whatever way doubt comes to you it will only disrupt your peace and calm.

Do something to counteract it by asking for help in prayer to see the depth of your doubt; 'the whys and wherefores', or, ask a question that may bring an answer to dissolve the doubt, for otherwise it will eat away at you, scattering the sacred moments of your life, which will never return.

You also need to clear doubt for the sake of others. If you doubt someone and do not give them a chance to explain, then you are being disrespectful to them and 'hanging them without a trial'. Is that wise or a spiritual way to do things?

There is a reason for everything. I believe in giving everyone the benefit of the doubt in every way, until I know the reason behind what they say or do. This goes for our family, children, partner as well. We may not always like the reason that they may give, but if it's a reason of *truth*, then *that* reason given will help us to complete our thoughts on what the doubt was all about, hopefully changing the negative energy of doubt into a positive energy of understanding and acceptance.

To Solve Addictions

Pray and ask for the strength to give the said addiction up.

Many people I know of have found that sincere prayer works.

✦

Some people find that taking a Healing or Counselling course

also works by giving them something to aspire to.

✦

Pure Meditation practised regularly with devotion

has saved many souls from an addiction of one form or another.

✦

If we ourselves master an addiction then it will not trouble us

again ~ unless we pause to look, remember,

and open the door to it by tempting it back.

✦

If it is karmic we have to work through it, and by doing so

strengthen ourselves, bringing a greater learning

by which we may help others.

Alcohol -
Spirit and The Spiritual

We do not have to forsake all things of a mortal nature whilst on the spiritual path, in fact if we gave everything up without a more serious thought, the 'giving up' may not last. Slowly but surely is the most secure way to give up most things so there are no side effects to jolt the body and being. There are always exceptions whereby it can be done instantaneously, but they are rare rather than the norm.

Alcohol and spirit substances are not good for you for many different reasons. They give you a feeling of wellbeing and exuberance, only to leave you after a period of time on a 'downer'. Too much consumed will affect the liver and possibly other organs thus affecting our lifespan. The most serious effect it will have on sensitive people who meditate ~ who are 'open' ~ will be an imbalance of their energies, opening them up to the psychic power of a lower energy force which can cause much harm to their minds and bodies.

More people need to know of this truth and so save themselves many very unpleasant problems, least of all that of bad behaviour and bad language.

If a person does not have a problem of addictiveness, then one glass of wine sipped with a meal from time to time will not harm them. Pure spirits like whisky and brandy, unless taken when needed on medicinal grounds, are harmful to the 'open' sensitive person and should not **ever** be indulged in.

Infinite Beloved

I surrender to my Higher Self ~ God

all actions and the outcome

of my deeds, so that I can be

truly at ONE with you

my Infinite Beloved.

*Thy **Will Be Done***

Surrender
and Let God Work Through You

To some people surrendering to God means losing their identity. Not So! It means saying "Thy Will" or 'let the will of Life be done" ~ going with the flow of what comes to you, taking it up with neither worry nor any concern, working with whatever it is, in the wisest way that you can and surrendering the *outcome* to God.

For God *knows*

Surrender as such, will bring you peace ~ peace of the mind. It is surrendering also our WILL to *our* Higher Self's will.

It is not sitting back and doing nothing. you have to do your homework, but you surrender the OUTCOME. That is the important part to do ~ and truly mean it. This way you are opening the door of the Divine Power to help you find the correct answer in your life and to all happenings.

You cannot get to Self~Realization without doing this.

One day you will need to.

Why not NOW and see the great difference it makes to your life and those around you.

Surrender to Receive

Once we were perfect beings

at one with all

No separation.

'Till we fell from the purity of grace,

allowing pride and ego to enter,

causing us fear and sadness,

Separating ourselves from the

Divinity

of

the

God

WITHIN

Separation

There is no separation, except that which you make yourself ~ in your mind.

You are part of the whole. Part of all the life force.

All peoples are linked together by an invisible cord of creative energy. We are all brothers and sisters, each having traits, personality or suchlike, that can also be found in many other people. You have known many souls before, in another lifetime and forget on rebirth, only to remember again when we meet someone whom we take a liking to, or, feel we have known them before or know them well on meeting ~ a familiar voice, face, personality ~ just a *knowing* feeling within.

Whether you take to some people or not is beside the point, you are *still* linked. This is why it is so important to realize this. Not all will become your friends, but all should be treated with respect ~ and not disdain for people that you do not care for.

You cannot separate God from yourself ~ for God is within you, though you can close the door on the God within.

You make your own separation from people ~ God ~ all of life.

Once you see there is no separation, then you can understand why we should love and respect our God~like self and others, however bad, who have that God-like kernel somewhere deep within them ~ with or without knowledge of this.

You cannot condone a bad or evil act by a person. We must though remember the Godlike kernel deep within them and pray for its Realization

God only

knows the whole truth.

When completely at ONE with God

we shall know the truth.

'Till then we can only struggle

to know part of the whole

that we are allowed to see

~ whilst realizing that all spiritual (God's)

mysteries are not solvable ~ now.

PRAY

God only in my heart and soul

My will is thy will

So help me God.

"God Only."
"Thy Will is My Will."

Two affirmations to be said night and morning. Say them with deep sincerity. Say them quietly to yourself, inwardly, during the day until you find that you are living these *very* words.

There is **God** only nothing else matters, for God's life force is in everything. We live and fall by the Grace of the Infinite Beloved ~ within our Higher Self.

I am here to guide you, help you, and love you unconditionally, but do remember I am only here to help you find your own true self ~ the 'God within'. Listen to the wisdom, but give your devotion to God alone. God is love, peace, joy, light eternal. There is a storehouse of all your needs just waiting for you.

"Seek ye first the Kingdom of Heaven (the God within) and all shall be added unto you."

I have done this and found it to be so true, liberating beyond belief ~ fulfilling all my needs.

There is no reality ~ all is a dream, except God. The one Infinite Power that we can rely on, trust, and rest in ~ in times of happiness and distress ~ is God's Divine Power.

Why suffer, worry and make life more difficult ~ when you have a *hand* to guide you, a loving light to hold you and surround you.

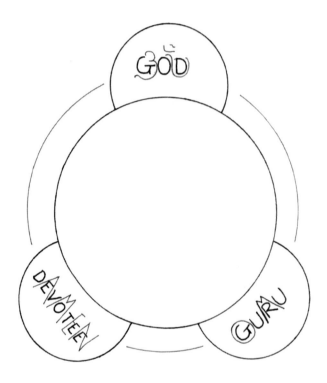

Communication
by God~Guru and Disciple

If a devotee~disciple of Pure Meditation is truly in need, they have but to ask for help for this need, putting God~Guru into their third eye, holding their image in mind, quietly asking within for help. This needs to be held until you feel at peace and feel that your need has been heard. Make not demands of any kind ~ no time factor ~ and then go about your day's work.

Your thought, which is energy, will instantaneously be received and whatever is best for yourself and progress of the mind body and spirit will come about.

"Not my will
but Thy Will be done."

I use this spiritual and scientific method for most of my dealings with God's worldwide devotees.

Jesus and the Master Gurus have always known of this form of communication ~

better by far

quicker in nature

the truth on receiving.

Love changes all

Hate changes nothing

Pray *to* change

and see

how *you* and *they*

will

change

Breaking The Cycle
of Hate and Distrust

Sadly I have to say that there are not many people that one can completely trust, though we should put our trust in everyone until proved otherwise, for, trust can often 'beget' trust.

Hate and distrust of others *can* mean we do not like or trust ourselves at base, also these feelings have an energy of their own ~ a very disruptive one, though by breaking and changing this cycle within us, we can change this bad energy into good useful energy without loss of energy within.

If you do not have preconceptions of people and how they should be and act, then, you can't be 'let down'. If someone cannot be trusted, you can still respect the omnipresent Divinity deep within that person, whilst taking care of how much trust you can give them.

The knowledge that they are not trustworthy will *set you free* to deal honestly with the matter in hand, knowing that one day in one lifetime, they will be trustworthy. Try to help them rather than hinder them, thereby furthering your own progress as well as theirs.

Most people say they hate this or that, or a person, when they really mean dislike. Hate is a very deep difficult emotion that is not natural for a human being to feel.

The best way to remedy hate/dislike is to remember that there is good in everybody ~ look for that *goodness*. Give them the benefit of the doubt and look towards changing this feeling/ energy into understanding, compassion and even love.

Pray for the person and yourself to change in thought.

I have often known people's hate/dislike of another change from dislike to like and then even to love.

Whatever you do ~ do not harbour this bad energy. Change it into a good energy before it does untold harm to your mind, body and spirit.

Speculation

Without

Knowledge

is

Dangerous.

Knowledge

Sets you

Free

Education and Travel are Important

Education in its broadest sense is not only about learning how to read, write, how to calculate figures and so forth. Education is most important when it comes to the learning of respect for others, how to give and receive; building one's character up, and above all bringing each individual up in a spiritual way to appreciate *all* of life.

Travel helps us to meet with other people of different nationalities, all so different, yet so alike. Travel should give us an understanding and acceptance of the country, its' ways, and also its' peoples, humbly showing us that we are not the only people on this earth plane with love, wisdom and good ideas.

So many facets of one's self need to be educated through birth, growing up, schooling, marriage and work to name but a few. Life itself is a big educator, one of the best.

What does it profit a person if they are clever, with wit and brains, if they do not learn how to live, how to cultivate peace and love within? How to sit quietly imbibing the creative power and energy of life? How to interact and interrelate with other people? *They do not truly profit.*

A solid broad-minded spiritual upbringing of respect, truth, honesty, love~peace~joy coupled with a good schooling and travel would be the ideal way forward.

So yes education and travel are of importance.

But put God and a spiritual upbringing first and foremost.

Smile at Yourself

Look in the mirror,
Pull a face at yourself
and continue until it makes you smile.

Then you are half way there

Try telling a funny story about yourself
and a mishap
If you can smile - and - *they* can

You are three-quarters there

If you can find humour in all of life
Then you are one hundred percent there.

Help yourself to humour,
Help others to humour.

A laugh ~ a smile ~ good humour

can help cure our ills.

Finding Balance ~ With Humour

Humour plays a very important part in one's approach to life and how we want to live.

Not everyone has a sense of humour; if not, it is worth cultivating and can be cultivated to some degree.

Humour between people or within a person on their own, will deflect the sting in most trivial problems of the mind, and lower intensity within one's self with the issues of much larger problems, thereby finding a balance within our being. This in turn gives us a different perspective, and allows us to find a wiser solution to whatever the problem may be.

We need to be able to laugh at ourselves and laugh *with* other people.

Have you noticed how often people can find humour at others expense, but, not at their own. Why not our own? Do we fear our pride and ego will be hurt?

Let it be hurt ~ it's good for it, and for us to be humble enough to accept our 'funny failings' or 'funny bits'.

Humour is very freeing, very liberating providing it does not contain harm or sarcasm.

There's an old true saying:

> 'Laugh and the world laughs with you,
> Cry and you cry alone'

Cultivate humour and MAKE THE WORLD LAUGH.

Please Help Me!

I know all knowledge is in the ether

all knowledge is accessible

~

May I attune myself to this knowledge,

and through my higher intuition,

find the answer that I am seeking.

~

So truth and wisdom prevail

in all that I say, think, and do.

Attunement

Attunement is *tuning in* to a person, place, or thing, to harmonise with it, and receive an intuitive feeling about what that person, place or thing needs. Intuitiveness is having perfect peace ~ with the attunement and knowledge felt by you. When I was touring and working in America, Hong Kong and the Phillippines, I attuned myself to each country ~ its' differences, also to the people by attuning myself to their words, actions and unspoken thoughts. This was a great help as often the people I spoke to did not speak any English ~ or very little

Doing the same in New Zealand, Australia and other countries I found myself understanding them and their concepts very well, if I had not 'attuned' I do believe many misunderstandings could have taken place, particularly with the usage of words.

I remember in downtown Los Angeles, in America, when my car was parked near a water hydrant (what I didn't know at the time was that one can be fined for this) someone gesticulated wildly to me speaking in another language that I could not understand. Whilst he was flinging his arms about and shouting from a second floor window, I tuned into his mind and realised that he was not angry but wanted to help me, and then picked up intuitively what he was trying to tell me. This was just one instance, though in my travels, my meetings were often with unusual people and unusual incidents occurred more often than not. But as is well known, wherever one is, even in parts of England, Scotland or Ireland, dialect and words are not always easily understood.

I give my humble thanks to attunement and intuition.

We can 'tune' into people and animals, in fact all of life this way.

For example, firstly we need to *desire* to expand our knowledge of that person, language, or animal. Secondly concentrate deeply into the brow centre with this thought, picturing it if possible, though this is not entirely necessary. Keep this concentration until you are attuned and 'pick up' on whatever you need to know; have faith and you will.

Attunement~attuning is very important for doctors, nurses, all therapists, in fact, we should all learn this art.

It is never too late to learn.

The Guru

A Guru is often feared ∼ for their light,

Stoned for their WISDOM,

trampled upon ∼ for their deity,

yet, loved inwardly ∼ unreservedly

by the spirit of that person.

Be they harsh ∼ be they soft

God's will and unconditional love

is their only Reason.

What is a Guru?
How can they help you?

Guru means one who dissolves the darkness and reveals all truths. A Spiritual Guide.

They volunteer to come back to this earth plane for many different reasons, each with their own special work to perform.

They are there to spread unconditional love, peace, truth and light to all who are ready and willing to receive.

Gurus *feel* God within and are at one with the Divine Power, therefore, there is nothing that they need from you, or ask of you, except that you come and receive. You need to go with respect for the truth and to listen to their wisdom. Do not try to hide behind an untruth or hide your true or false self, for they will know and be aware of this situation.

Many defile the name Guru or Master, for they fear that which they do not know. Sad for they gain nothing and lose much.

They do not desire anything except the welfare of the human soul and are there to help those in need to find their true SELVES ~ their true identity. To guide you to finding peace, joy, and love in this lifetime. To find the **God within** and God Realization ~ Self~Realization.

Such a person is not to be trivialised or taken lightly.

We cannot be perfect

in this life

but

We can *try*

What Is and Makes
a Good Christian?

I see 'Christian' as being a more embracing word than is generally accepted. Christians are not necessarily only people who are religious church–goers, they truly are not all Christians in the correct sense of the word.

Firstly what is a Christian, by definition? Broadly and in spiritual context it means a person that believes in the Christ Power, a Christ-ian (person.) It should also mean a person of good content ~ a Christ~believer.

So what makes a good Christian? One who believes there is a Christ power. One who practises the truths of the Christ Power, that of truth, honesty, prayer, love, giving of their time and self to help others in whatever way is needed. Sometimes this can just be being a mother and looking after her children. There are many different ways.

A good Christian is of joy for they know God is of peace, love and joy.

Some think and say that they are a Christian whilst thinking bad/evil thoughts ~ they are *not*.

Others feel unworthy ~ thinking good thoughts ~ they *are*.

Which are you?

Knowledge sets us free,

then,

we need with wisdom

TO

act on that knowledge.

Be Thankful ~ Be Truthful

Many times people will grumble over their lack of money, health, clothes, friends, yet, do they ever give thanks for what they do have ~ for being alive, having time to accomplish, time to work out any karma, if needs be.

So many people around us can be so much worse off than ourselves. Do we ever think about this and then give thanks to God sincerely from our heart for **all** that we have?

If we can hear, see, smell, walk, talk, be able to use our arms and hands - we are fortunate. If we then lose a leg we should be grateful we *have* all but that one leg. Whatever we have *not* got, we should *still* be grateful for what we have. It may not be much but that does not stop our giving thanks for what is left.

Whatever happens to me I always find something to rejoice over ~ there is always *something* if you wish to find it.

There is duality in everything in life. We have spiritual recompense for anything that is lost of our body or mind. We get compensated in one way or another. You may not see this, or wish to, but if you do ~ and look carefully you will find this to be true.

A true fact is that the people who have most to complain about ~ do not. Those who have the least to complain about ~ do complain the most.

Be grateful ~ thank God ~ and be happy.

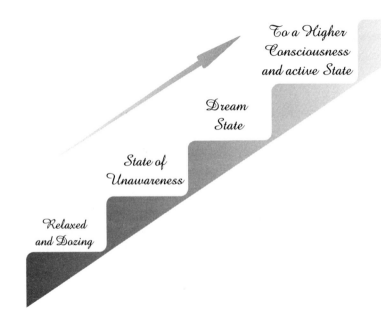

Dreams

People often ask me if dreams are important, and do they mean anything. Yes, they do ~ we need them like we need to sleep.

Many problems, some karma, and a testing of how we are and would react in life are some of the important aspects of dreaming. Some dreams of course are nonsense, they come from watching TV programmes or an argument that has taken place.

If we are meant to remember a specific dream we will wake up with it very clearly imprinted on our mind and it will stay there for us to look at and decipher. These are the most important ones for us to receive as often they can warn us before a disaster that may not need to take place.

Once this happened to me. The dream was of a tyre of my car bursting whilst driving. The next day the tyres were checked and there was found to be a bad fault in one of the tyres; an accident was prevented.

I do not believe it's necessary to spend hours pondering the dreams we have, also, it is very difficult to interpret most of them, unless you have the ability from a past life and are spiritually highly intuitive. I'm not saying that it is impossible ~ but difficult to get it right ~ yes.

In the *first stage before sleep*, we find a relaxed, dozing or half awake feeling, where often we are thinking. At this stage problems can be answered and creative thinking can flow.

The *stage of unawareness* is where a thought stays, if needed, to be remembered upon our awakening.

The *dream state* as I have mentioned can be for us to work things out of different kinds, or for 'nonsense' dreams.

The fourth stage is where our spirit comes more into focus ~ much deeper work is done here.

You will never feel free,

and completely at peace,

until you know

and love God,

the Infinite Beloved,

in deep devotion

with

all your heart

and soul.

How to Know and Love God

How do you love your lover? With devotion, commitment, loyalty, unconditional love and *complete* faith in that one person.

So it should be in the same way that you love God, for, God can be impersonal or personal, depending on your depth of unconditional love and faith ~ and also on your needs. One thing is certain that God loves *you*.

We have to be able to love, so we have family and friends to practice with, then, perhaps later on in life we are fortunate we find a spiritual guide ~ Guru to respect and love, but it is not for their 'visage' or personality that we should love them, but the wisdom and truths that they have to offer you.

If you can love your Guru as you should love God ~ then you *will* love God. No imposed conditions, no demands imposed, for love is about giving, not receiving.

It is easy to love God when we count our blessings and see the beauty in all of nature; the *good* things we have received, and we do receive even more, with this profound love and faith that I pray you will have or be blessed with.

God sends Masters and Gurus because the One God knows how difficult it is for you to love the omnipresent *One*, whereby it is easier to do so with the 'messenger' and through loving that 'messenger' will find how to know and love God.

Unconditional Love ~ Faith are the passwords.

Modern~day Appliances
Do Affect Us

Anything of energy must give out energy ~ so it stands to reason and in using any terminology for it, that energy in whatever forms used, can help, but at the same time can hinder with its' side effects.

For example, T.V, computers, mobile phones and such like are not good for us, and should be used sparingly when possible. They can be particularly harmful for people who are on a spiritual path, meditate, those people whose chakras are *well* open. The side effects of too much usage can bring on irritability, restlessness, lethargy and headaches. I know these appliances are here to stay and are on the increase, no doubt in years to come our body and mind will change in various ways to accept this influx. I'm not so certain about the spirit ~ the advancing SOUL ~ I do not believe it will, so the problem is what to do!

With positive mind and balancing your energies, only using these appliances when needed, you will, with this knowledge, be able to prevent harm being done.

Sex and violence in films does affect us whatever we may think. Try not to watch such films, or lower your eyes if it is not possible to do otherwise.

Our hearing ~ our sight ~ our minds ~ are in jeopardy here.

We soak up events, details, the spoken word and actions in our subconscious, where all can manifest there. Do we want the violence of rape, murder, sex to be dormant there? We see this outcome in some people, when these acts are played out in reality, yet nothing gets done about it.

Our minds are there to absorb and use our experiences to good effect in our lives.

If it absorbs these, then it will absorb everything, though few will admit to this, for to do so, they feel would spoil their entertainment.

It's not the appliances that are to be blamed as much as how they are used, gaining knowledge of them in relation to ourselves, and what we *need*.

Knowledge ~ Wisdom

to

Balance ~ then use.

I WILL

Give me the strength to find my way,

to feel more joy every day.

❖ ❖ ❖

My spirit is weak but yours is strong,

cradle me in your arms all day long.

❖ ❖

I say a prayer

Doing all I can

Knowing that you are near

❖

I shall *be well*

I shall *do well*

That is what *I* hear

So be it.

Depression, Despair
~ Maya and Illusion

If we are in pain and we fall asleep, we do not feel the pain we had when awake, so we have to ask ourselves *why* we do not feel it when asleep? The mind has not been relaying the message of pain. If we have a pain and the house was on fire, the pain would be forgotten, while the all~powerful mind kept us busy with the fire, so, therefore is the pain there?
It it real ~ or illusory?

All of life is of Maya ~ an illusion, made to seem real by our mind power. We can produce a headache, pain, or no pain or headache. I remember when very young if I didn't want to attend school I would produce a headache and *real* sickness, likewise my mind could reverse it.

Our minds can be used for the good or not so good, to benefit our life or not, it is therefore up to us to decide and use the positive mind power that we all have.

Depression and despair can also be helped with the power- ful mind. We need to harness that power and use it construc- tively.

Use the affirmation:

"I am getting better every day in every way!"

Though we must acknowledge our despair or depression, we must not allow it to enter our thoughts so that it will stay; in fact quite the reverse. *For* God *does not want us to be like this.*

You have a soul, a spirit, and a powerful mind. Acknowledge these powerful weapons. Pray, affirm you *are* getting more joyful. Deny all negative thoughts by finding a positive answer to them. You need to exercise; walk, swim and find work to occupy your mind.

When we are in distress our breathing becomes much shallower ~ we take in less of the oxygen that keeps our lungs

Help Us

Infinite Beloved

We forget that our body
is the vessel
for the Christ Power and Holy Spirit.

Help us to remember.

We forget how perfectly our
bodies are made,
and how well they work for us,
if we look after them.

Help us to remember.

We forget how a positive mind
can help a body overcome any of its dis-eases.

Infinite Beloved

Help us to remember

filled and our body and brain oxygenated, so do some proper breathing in the open air each day.

Put both your hands on your ribcage and move your hands gently outwards helping your ribs to expand as you breathe deeply. Do not do this too often to begin with as the intake of much more oxygen could make you feel a little 'giddy'. Work up slowly doing three breaths to begin with, and so on, using your common sense and intuitiveness ~ and see how it benefits you.

I know you may need help to start with, be it with medical assistance, counselling or other therapies, but eventually it comes down to **you** to help **yourself**.

All medication has side effects, so do come off them as soon as you feel able to. You will need 'will power' for this ~ prayer and positive thought.

The respect and strength derived from helping your Self will amaze you ~ and stay with you to feed you for the rest of your life.

STAY with this knowledge.

✡

✡

All Ages

Respect

and

Love

should

with

treated

be

What is Age?

Age is how we tell approximately where we are in our life's span.

Age of itself is not important, and is best forgotten about, for too much thought on the subject makes us not only beholden to our age ~ but possibly also makes us feel it. It would not be sensible, though, for a person to say that age is unimportant altogether.

From a person's age we have a rough idea of where they should be 'at' ~ for job interviews, for dentists and doctors appointments for example. This information is of importance. On the other hand, our body can look one age and our minds can be another ~ hence the expression "you are as old as you feel."

Do not put too much importance on age, but use it as a 'yard stick' only.

Keep your mind and body active.

Being young in heart

is to be young forever.

I Pray for Forgiveness

for

any harm that I may have done

consciously or unconsciously to others.

I pray to my **Self** for forgiveness.

To have patience, understanding,

and give unconditional love to those

that do harm to myself and others.

Help me to see

that the Christ Power and Holy Spirit is within us all

Aum.

Meet Adversity with Love

Whatever people may think of you ~ good or bad ~ be they friends, relations or just casual acquaintances ~ give them of your love.

The more people hurt you or speak against you, bear no grudge ~ do not speak ill of them, for "they know not what they do." Try to understand them ~ the mortal part they reflect and come from ~ show them this understanding, and show them love, if they allow you to, and you can find it in your heart to do so.

It takes two to fight - life is too short. You can't always agree and often you may have to 'beg to differ'. Is this not the best way ~ the spiritual way ~ forwards? We do not and must not retaliate against those that harm us by word or deed, because

"What you sow you reap."

Our sins always find us out. Leave it to conscience and the God Within, then you do no harm to your **self** and reap no karma.

Many say they find it difficult to forgive and stay loving. I believe it is easy if you have no expectations of anyone ~ take them at the level of life that they are, remember them in your prayers ~ send them love and light for it is very easy to fall from the grace of truth, peace and unconditional love.

Look at where you may have had a part to play ~ if there is one.

Remember we are all souls of the Infinite Beloved.

What is Reality?

Life is a stage. We are the actors ~ acting out our part in this *seemingly* real drama. It all seems so real at the time, though, as each act finishes so another begins ~ overflowing from one *learning* to another, to build and shape us ~ one facet of one *life time* for *us* to fulfil.

Our bodies, vessels for the spirit, are made up of countless genes, cells, hormones, also cells and hormones on the move, and the heart, liver and kidneys all participating in our bodily functions and life within. At the same time the spirit tries to raise itself so that our spiritual side becomes uppermost. And yet ~ we are born to die ~ to pass from this earth plane ~ our soul soars whilst our body goes back to dust, to the earth.

Our bodies are transitory ~ our souls are forever.

Bricks and mortar, wood, fibres, and all so-called man-made solids perish at some time ~ there is no permanancy, yet such store is put upon them. Money is needed to live by, though having too much money changes people and it can become the 'root of all evil', changing people drastically in so many ways. One way being the worry over where to place the money to make more; another being that they may lose it and their lifestyle; even become *mean* in mind and to others, except to their own family.

There is no security in life, be it with money, with possessions, or with people.

Maybe we need less of the mortal 'trappings' to receive more of the spiritual ones

It seems only by our struggles with dis-ease, and the many problems that life brings, do we look within to find God and our True Selves.

There is only THE truth that ALL comes into being and passes except the spirit ~ the soul which is everlasting.

There is no security, except the unconditional love and light of GOD.

So why take this life so seriously? It was given to us to enjoy, to love, to have peace within, and above all to know that our life is but...

one act in the theatre of life.

Beloved ones of Light,

The Christ has risen

Within YOU.

See this fact~ realize it and rejoice

For as you accept,

so will you allow

the Christ Power to rise

and show itself even more.

The Second Coming of Christ

Some religions say that the second coming of Christ has happened. Other religions say that it is to come, whilst yet again some say that it is already here with us.

This is a much misunderstood biblical saying.

'The second coming of Christ is already here within us.'

Jesus came once again, another Master, son of God, to say that we are doomed if we do not change our ways, that the whole world would suffer. These words are not put in the bible, as I write them, but, they are there behind his words of wisdom and in many of his actions. Jesus said in his sermons that we need to look at our selves, change our bad habits, and above all get to know God. He knew we all were sons and daughters of the Infinite Beloved. That God was within. Jesus also knew that much of the wisdom spoken by him would fall on 'stony ground'. Still, we are all souls ~ loved unconditionally by God's unqualified bounty.

The second coming of Christ means that people will feel an awakening within (the Christ power) to look within. We shall want more knowledge and be aware there is more to life than just mortal pursuits.

Frustration, unease of the spirit wishing to raise its SELF will be felt. Evolution. Energy of pure light and love which the Christ Power is ~ will raise itself even more so within us and the Holy Spirit within will manifest and do.

The Christ is raised, we shall be torn apart if we do not see and acknowledge that this is truly happening.

In marriages, partnerships, families, countries, there will be much separation taking place, because it will be seen that some souls will want to progress with this 'awakening' and others will disregard it with fatal results to themselves.

We are in the early stages of being made aware of this

So it was written

There is no time for delay

The Time is Now

The second coming of Christ

IS HERE

The Holy Spirit will take up

The call

TO ACTION ~ for the good

of all humankind

SO BE IT.

Christ Power.

There is a quickening in every sense of the word in life.

We need to look within, purify, perfect our SELVES, so that we become better people ~ more God~like. Able to raise our light energy vibrations, so that we do not fall by the wayside by not being able to stand the full light and potency of the Christ power as it raises its SELF within...as

it will ~ for it is Time

It must do ~ to help save the human race.

My dear worldwide Souls,

I do not expect the truth to be easily accepted,
neither do I expect, if the truth written here is
accepted, that it will be acted upon immediately.
However one day, slowly and surely, the light of
wisdom will raise its head within each and every
one, enabling the way forwards,
seeing how best to act out these truths.

Prayer and Faith will guide you.

Mata Yogananda
Mahasaya Dharma

INDEX

Abortion	31	Change	4
Acceptance	192	Changing	
Addiction	194,195	the world	125
Adversity	231	Chasing	
Affirmations	201, 224, 225	your tail	67
Age	229	Child prodigies	191
Alcohol	195	Choice	112, 118, 119
Animals	98, 99	Christ	103, 235
Appliances	222	Christ Power	103, 215, 226
Arms of			235
the family	259	Christian	215
Astral plane	144	Cinema	222
Attunement	211	Clairvoyance	137
		Clairvoyant	137
Babies	17, 18	Cleansing	184
Bad habits	28	Common sense	179
Bad health	112	Communication	203
Bad posture	89	Communities	115
Balance	53, 95, 209	Computers	222
Be thankful	217	Concentration	160, 161
Beauty	6	Conception	17
Belief	87	Conscience	158, 159
Boyfriend	129	Consciousness	219
Breath	227	Conserving	
Broadminded	207	energy	59
		Constipation	165
Can I change		Cosmic	
the world?	125	consciousness	144
Cats	98	Country karma	184, 185
Causal plane	144	Covering over	59
Chakras	177	Creation	85

Death	155, 189, 232	Flirtation	35
Depression	225	Flowers	100
Desire	127	Food	131, 151, 165
Despair	225	Forgiveness	230
Devotee	203	Freedom	127
Diets	131	Friends	51
Disasters	185	Fun	163
Disciple	203	Funny	163
Disease	39, 47, 165		
Distrust	205	Gay	167
Divorce	69	Gifted children	191
Doctors	109	Girlfriend	129
Dogma	105	God	26, 67, 93, 203
Doubt	193	God alone	201
Dreams	219	God is within	82
Drinking	195	God only	201
Dying	155	God within	201
		Good health	112
Education	207	Good posture	89
Energy	222	Grief	155
Envy	7	Guru	203, 212, 213, 221
Exceptional talents	191		
		Habits	28
		Happy marriage	9
Faith	102, 193	Hate	205
Faith in yourself	183	Healing	59
		Healing power	59
The Fall	198	Health	112
Family	51	Hearing	149
Fasting	147, 149, 151	Hermit	115
Fasting from sound	149	Higher consciousness	219
Fasting from words	147	Holy Spirit	235, 236
		Homosexual	167
Fear	12, 13, 14	How can a Guru Help?	213
Films	222		

How can I change the world? 125
How can I find God? 93
How can I know God? 221
How to Love God? 221
Humour 163, 209

Illness 39, 165
Illusion 225
Infatuation 21
Insomnia 152
Intellect 179
Intelligence 179
Intuition 211

Jealousy 175
Jesus 103, 231
Jesus Christ 103
Jobs 37
Judgement 121

Karma 39, 42, 43, 121, 122, 184, 185
Knowledge 5, 216
Kriya 83
Kriya Yoga 83

Laugh 161, 209
Leisure time 95
Lesbian 167
Life 135, 181, 232

Life after death 189
Life is for living 91
Love 21, 23

Many mansions 155
Marriage 9, 10, 76, 77, 78
Mass karma 184, 185
Master 103, 221
Master souls 103
Masters 103, 221
Masturbation 166
Mata Yogananda XV
Mataji XV
Maya 225
Mean 232
Meaning of life 27
Medical profession 109
Medication 39, 110
Medicine 110
Meditation 27, 55, 81, 257
Meditation Evenings 257
Meditative state 81
Medium 137
Mediumship 137
Mind 63
Mind power 63
Miscarriages 31
Mobile phones 222
Money 232
Monk 115

Near death experience	189	Respect	24, 25, 98, 99, 180
Nuns	115	Responsibility	113
Omnipresent	73	Right choice	118, 119
One	199		
Oneness	85, 199	Saints	92, 103, 116
Order	115	Second coming of Christ	234, 235
Pain	40, 46, 47, 225	Security	65, 232
Partner	129	Security in life	65
Passing	155, 189	Self	5
Peace	106	Self~Realization	103
Peace makers	106	Self knowledge	127
Pills	39	Self mastery	127
Plants	101	Self Realization Meditation Healing Centre	XV, 253
Positivity	225		
Posture	89		
Prayer	8, 18, 73, 117	Self respect	25
Premonition	219	Separation (Marriage)	69
Prodigies	191		
Psychic	137	Separation from God	199
Pure Meditation	27, 55, 81, 120 131, 257	Sexual relations	79
		Side effects	110
Raja	83	Silence	147
Raja Yoga	83	Sinners	92, 116
Rape	97	Sleep	152
Reap	43, 44, 231	Sleepless Nights	152
Rebirth	189	Smile	208, 209
Recluse	115	Soul	232
Reincarnation	105	Soul mate	23
Relations	51	Sound	149
Religion	28, 103	Sow	43, 44, 231
Rely on yourself	183	Speech	147
		Spiritual eye	144, 145
Repentance	121, 123	Spiritual food	131

Spiritual law	121		Unreality	232
Stillness	147			
Suffering	40		Verbal fasting	147
Suicide	171			
Surrender	196, 197		What are we	
			here for?	27
Taking a life	171		What is a	
Taking			Guru?	213
responsibility	113		What is God?	93
Talent	190, 191		What we sow	
Talking to plants	101		we reap	43, 231
Television	222		Where is God?	93
Tension	227		Why are we	
Third eye	144, 145, 203		here?	27
Thought	84, 87, 139		Why?	135
Thy will			Wisdom	103
be done	201		Work	37
Tragedies	185			
Travel	207, 211		Yang	52, 53
True love	23		Yin	52, 53
True self	49		Yoga	83
Trustworthy	205		You are special	57
Truth	1, 162, 217		Youth	229
Turn the				
other cheek	107			
T.V.	222			

The Self Realization Meditation Healing Centre

The Self Realization Meditation Healing Centre was founded in the Ether, then in the heart of Mata Yogananda. The Centres' given emblem of the 'I am' is shown on all the Self Realization Meditation Healing Centre material ~ so that people may know that they are dealing authentically with the Centre.

For information on Pure Meditation, Natural Spiritual Healing, Progressive Counselling and other courses, please contact:

Self Realization Meditation Healing Centre

Laurel Lane, Queen Camel, Yeovil, Somerset, BA22 7NU, UK.
Tel. 01935 850266   Fax. 01935 850234

Internet: http://www.selfrealizationcentres.org
E-mail: info@selfrealizationcentres.org

Sister Centres:

New Zealand - South Island
100 Highsted Road, Bishopdale,
Christchurch, New Zealand
Ph. 03 359 8507   Fax. 03 359 3430

Canada
RR9 736 Creekside Crescent,
Gibsons Landing B.C., V0N 1V9,
Canada Tel. & Fax. (604) 886 0898

Australia Contact:
Balangara, Farrer Road, Mount Wilson
N.S.W, 2786, Australia.
Tel/Fax. 02 4756 2042
Mobile 0415 543473

USA Contact:
7187 Drumheller Road, Bath, MI 48808
USA. Ph. & Fax. (517) 641–6201

Switzerland and Germany contact: Dorfgasse 76 (Schoren),
CH–4900 Langenthal, Switzerland.
Tel. 062 922 8187 Fax. 062 922 8127

Beliefs and Aims of the Centre

1. The spreading of the truth.
2. That there is no death, only organised life.
3. That scientific and spiritual knowledge lead to Self~Realization, peace and harmony.
4. To bring harmony to the mind, body and spirit of all God's living creatures.
5. To show that *LOVE* is the strongest energy force that there is, anywhere.
6. To show that all people and all religions will lead eventually to the one and same pathway, to Self~Realization and God.
7. That knowledge will dispel ignorance and fear and make us whole.
8. To provide pure thoughts to beget high minds.
9. To find our true selves through Pure Meditation.
10. To rid ourselves of all negative states of the mind and body.
11. To spread unconditional love throughout the world.
12. To uphold the wisdom of the Masters, such as Jesus, Babaji, Buddha and the Saints.
13. To prove that there are many Masters and many Man-sions ~ for us all.

BUT ONLY ONE GOD.

❂ Light Up The World! ❂
Meditation Evenings Worldwide

*to bring souls together to imbibe and go forward
to Self~Realization*

It was with great joy that the first Open Meditation evening was held at the Mother Centre many years ago; souls coming together to imbibe Divine Peace and Love, to seek Self~Realization through Pure Meditation. Since that time many Open Meditation evenings have come into being around the world ~ like stars of Love shining their light into the darkness of separation, delusion and suffering.

We hope that many more souls will be moved to open their hearts and their homes in this way, until the world is full of Light.

We look forward to you joining us ~ in the list below you will find your nearest Meditation Evening. Please ring for details.

These Meditation Evenings, and the Arms of the Family, are expanding all the time ~ please contact the UK Mother Centre for further details and contacts.

The peace~oneness in Meditation ~ joy for all to share.

UK Mother Centre

Somerset, Queen Camel ◆ Monday - Saturday 8.45 for 9pm Meditation
Sundays 7.45 for 8pm Meditation ◆ (01935) 850266

UK

Bath, Bathford ◆ Thursdays weekly, 8.30pm for 8.45pm Meditation
Wendy Allen ◆ (01225) 852550
Bristol, Pensford ◆ Mondays 8.30pm weekly
Julia Raffo and Michael Simmons ◆ (01761) 490556
Bristol, St. Andrews ◆ 8.30pm last Tuesday of each month
Lindy Gibbon ◆ (0117) 944 2711
Devon, Newton Abbott ◆ 7.45pm for 8pm Meditation, first Sunday
of each month ◆ Rowena Nicholson and Jason Hinrich ◆ (01803 872041)
Devon, South Molton ◆ 6.30 for 7pm Meditation,
first Thursday of each month Sarah Beanland ◆ (01598) 760592
London, W11 ◆ 8pm, first Tuesday of each month
Emma Ball ◆ (0207) 792 3715
Scotland, Edinburgh ◆ Saturdays, weekly, 8.45 for 9pm Meditation
Satay Singh ◆ (0131) 467 0828/Mobile 07811 853319
Somerset, Frome ◆ Mondays and Thursdays 8.30pm weekly and other times
by request ◆ Charles Kemp and Sara Crowley ◆ (01373) 462606
Somerset, Glastonbury ◆ Wednesdays, weekly 7.45 for 8pm Meditation
Carol and Terry Palmer ◆ (01458) 831353
Somerset, Martock ◆ 8.45 for 9pm Meditation, first Thursday of each month
Rossananda and Mahseeman Young ◆ (01935) 824142
Somerset, Wells ◆ 7.45 for 8pm Meditation, first Monday of each month
Joy Buchanan ◆ (01934) 712082
Wales, Brecon ◆ 7.30 for 8pm Meditation, first Monday of each month
Fee & Richard Curtis ◆ (01874) 624067
Yorkshire, Richmond ◆ 8.30pm first Wednesday of each Month
Maureen Clayton ◆ (01748) 886188

Australia

Blue Mountains, Katoomba area, ◆ Tuesdays 7.30pm weekly
Denis Daly ◆ 0415 543473

Meditation Evenings Worldwide

Canada

British Columbia, Gibsons Landing ◆ Monday-Saturday 8.45 for 9pm Meditation
Sundays 7.45 for 8pm Meditation ◆ Canadian Centre ◆ (604) 886 0898
British Columbia, Davis Bay ◆ Thursdays 8.45pm weekly
Nicole and Keith Bradford ◆ (604) 885 0977
British Columbia, North Vancouver ◆ 10.30am, third Sunday of each month
Noel Hanuse ◆ (604) 983 9661
British Columbia, Pender Harbour ◆ Mondays 7.45pm weekly
Carrie Sassarat and Keith Shaw ◆ (604) 883 9195

Germany

Baden-Wuerttemberg, Waldkirch ◆ Mondays 8.30pm weekly
Renate Schölz ◆ 7681 490792

New Zealand

South Island, Christchurch ◆ Monday-Saturday 8.45 for 9pm Meditation
Sundays 7.45 for 8pm Meditation Christchurch Centre ◆ (03) 359 8507
South Island, Nelson ◆ Sundays 7.45pm weekly
Paul and Victoria Woodward ◆ (03) 540 3970
North Island, Auckland ◆ Wednesdays 8.15 for 8.30pm first, third and fifth
Wednesday of each month ◆ Adriana Tuscia ◆ (09) 360 8616
North Island, Auckland & North Shore ◆ Wednesdays 8.15 for 8.30pm second
and forth Wednesday of each month Margaret Tabuteau ◆ (09) 445 3657
North Island, Rotorua ◆ Sundays 8.15 for 8.30pm weekly
Suzanne Meek ◆ (021) 107 1742
North Island, Warkworth (Matakana) ◆ Sundays 7.45 for 8pm first & third
Sunday of each month ◆ Colette Taylor ◆ (09) 422 5255
North Island, Wellington ◆ Sundays 7.45 for 8pm
Ràna Webster and Dev Verma ◆ (06) 378 0990

Switzerland

Langenthal ◆ Wednesdays 8.30pm weekly
Franziska Fischer ◆ 062 922 8187

USA

Michigan, Lansing ◆ Sundays 9.45am weekly
Betty Kronemeyer, Jenny and Scott Rowe ◆ (517) 641 6201

∾ Arms of the Family ∾

The Arms of the Family offer bed and breakfast and/or dinner to students/friends of the worldwide Self Realization Meditation Healing Centres: for those friends who are travelling and wish to find a loving place to rest their heads 'en route' and know that they will be welcome. In this way we hope to bring a sharing of life with those of a like mind.
Please ring the UK Mother Centre for further contacts and details.

UK
Bristol, Nailsea ✦ Roger Furneaux ✦ (01275) 853786
Bristol, Pensford ✦ Julia Raffo and Michael Simmons ✦ (01761) 490556
Essex, Clacton-on-Sea ✦ Geraldine and Paul Maitland-Edwards
(01255) 425113
Hampshire, New Forest ✦ Mike Barker and Lorraine Stephens
(02380) 814048
Somerset, Martock ✦ Rossananda and Mahseeman Young ✦ (01935) 824142
Somerset, Wells ✦ Joy and Alan Buchanan ✦ (01934) 712082
Somerset, Wyke Champflower (Nr. Bruton)
Noreen Daniel and Eileen Lemon ✦ (01749) 812788
Wales, Brecon ✦ Fee & Richard Curtis ✦ (01874) 624067
Wales, Brecon ✦ Gabelle and Michael Eisele ✦ (01874) 690116
Wales, Powys ✦ Mark Chappell ✦ (01686) 412307
Yorkshire, Richmond ✦ Maureen Clayton ✦ (01748) 886188

Canada
British Columbia, Pender Harbour ✦ Carrie Sassarat and Keith Shaw ✦ (604) 883 9195

New Zealand
South Island, Nelson ✦ Paul and Victoria Woodward ✦ (03) 540 3970
North Island, Wellington ✦ Ràna Webster and Dev Verma ✦ (06) 378 0990

Switzerland
Langenthal ✦ Franziska Fischer ✦ 062 922 8187

USA
Michigan, Lansing ✦ Betty Kronemeyer, Jenny and Scott Rowe
(517) 641 6201

All the Centres are here for you.
If you need further information of any kind, please do contact us.

Help us Help Others!

Dear Reader,

The Self Realization Meditation Healing Centre is a registered charity helping and guiding all. We teach Pure Meditation, train professional healers, counsellors and spiritual teachers, and offer retreats for those in need.

Much of our work involves helping those suffering from all forms of physical and mental illness, stress, and trauma.

You can help us to help people in need.

Any donation would make an enormous difference to our voluntary work and would be gratefully received.

Your total donation will go directly to:

• Help those in need receive Natural Spiritual Healing, Progressive Counselling, Pure Meditation and any other form of therapy that they need at the Centre.
• A bursary fund to help people take our self-help courses who cannot meet their full cost.

There are many other ways to help us ~ a Tithe Box (available at the Centres) and the Sustainers Fund. *Legacies are gratefully accepted.*

If you would like to receive further information on the above or on the Centre, please contact us :

Self Realization Meditation Healing Centre
Laurel Lane, Queen Camel, Yeovil, Somerset, BA22 7NU, UK.
Tel. 01935 850266   Fax. 01935 850234

Internet: http://www.selfrealizationcentres.org
E-mail: info@selfrealizationcentres.org

Your donation **will** make a difference

Thank you for reading.

Other Publications by Mata Yogananda available from Daoseva Press

Daoseva Press

Books

SELF~REALIZATION THROUGH MEDITATION *ISBN 09522734 7 0*
COME ~ a *Spiritual Journey* ISBN 0 9522734 5 4
POEMS OF THE HEART ISBN 0 9522734 9 7
SONG~SOUL CHANTS *ISBN 09522734 3 8*
SONG~SOUL CHANTS ("Small songbook")
SPIRITUAL FAMILIES AND CENTRES ~ an Unknown Journey
ISBN 09522734 0 3

Videos

~ *Imbibe in Mata Yogananda's wisdom ~ in person.*
Centres of Light
Talks With Mata Yogananda
A Message from Mata
Questions and Answers with Mata

Videos are supplied on cassette (VHS/PAL) Some are available in the NTSC format.
Please contact your nearest centre for details.

 DHARMA

Dharma is the Centres' yearly magazine presenting the Wisdom of God~Life and the Masters; with articles by Mata Yogananda and people in different professional fields including those in holistic health care. The emphasis is on practical spirituality, covering all aspects of life. Please contact the Centre to order the current issue of Dharma. Subscriptions (three and five year) and back issues are also available. ISSN 1366–3550

Photographs of Mata

We are delighted to now have available photographs of Mata in a beautiful glossy finish. Yours to treasure, these photos will bring Mata's light to your whole being.

Inspiring Talk Tapes *by Mata Yogananda*

Mata Yogananda talks on real life issues with love and understanding; of the difficulties we all must overcome in our progress back to consciousness of our spiritual nature. Mata has recorded this series of talks so that her words may reach out to those not able to be with her, and yet needing the encouragement and demonstration that it is possible to live a God~centred life in this world today.

Inspiring Talk Tapes are supplied on cassette or Compact Disc. Please enquire for further details.

⚶ *For all authentic publications of the Self Realization Meditation Healing Centre*
by Daoseva Press, please contact your nearest authorised dealer
or Centre for prices and availability. ⚶

May God be with you

On your journey